ROCK BOTTOM
BOTTOM
HAS A
TRAMPOLINE

ROCK BOTTOM HAS A TRAMPOLINE

How to Turn Every Loss into a Win
with the Like-Hearted Mentor™

CHARLYNDA SCALES

with Brunella Costagliola

ONBrand Books
an imprint of W. Brand Publishing
NASHVILLE, TENNESSEE

j.brand@wbrandpub.com

W. Brand Publishing

www.wbrandpub.com

Cover design: designchik.net

Cover imagery: Shutterstock

Ghostwriter: Brunella Costagliola

Copy Editor: Virginia Bhashkar

Rock Bottom Has a Trampoline —1st ed.

Available in Hardcover, Paperback, Kindle, and eBook formats.
Hardcover: 978-1-956906-68-4
Paperback: 978-1-956906-69-1
eBook: 978-1-956906-70-7

Library of Congress Control Number: 2023916901

CONTENTS

WHO IS THIS BOOK FOR?

You will hit rock bottom at one point or another in your entrepreneurial journey, and when you do, I don't want you to be caught off guard or feel alone. That is why I have written this book—your tool behind the glass that you can "break in case of an emergency."

I'm going to give it to you straight, starting with who I am. Most books are written after the author has "made it." They've already become a gazillionaire, they're famous and have the big house, and they're telling you how you can do it too. Me? Right now, I am a proud thousandaire. I have debt, I drive a Honda, and I'm decidedly sharing my story although I'm a single mother, I take care of my parents, I have like four jobs, and I barely kept my business afloat during the pandemic. I want to reach you while I'm still in the grind and I pray that my testimony helps you, because if I save just one person, then my journey and pain have served their purpose.

Just like me, you were not born to hit the ground and stay there. You have a gift and vision that was given to you. Often, it may feel like this journey is bigger than you, and that's because it is. Just like me, you are a messenger and a catalyst for something great. It's an honor to be a part of your journey and story.

This book is like the Choose Your Own Adventure books we enjoyed as children. You may only relate to one or two chapters now, but other parts could become very relevant to you later. And, by the insights you glean from these pages, you'll also become equipped to help others you may encounter who want to start, grow, or recover as business owners.

But first, if you've ever wondered if you can recover from what you are going through, remember that there is a blessing in being able to talk about rock bottom in the past tense, and you will get there.

Alright? Good; let's move on.

I offer this writing as a guiding light for individuals who have ventured into the challenging world of entrepreneurship and encountered their fair share of rock bottom moments; it has been tailored to provide insight, inspiration, and practical strategies for a diverse range of readers, as outlined below. As you read, consider which of these categories and benefits applies to you:

Emerging Entrepreneurs: If you are just starting your entrepreneurial journey, this book offers wisdom to anticipate and navigate the lows inherent in building a business from the ground up.

Struggling Business Owners: For the entrepreneur facing setbacks, financial hardships, or stalled growth, you will find solace in the stories and advice within this book, as you foster the resilience to overcome your adversity.

Mid-Career Professionals: If you are transitioning from a corporate role to entrepreneurship, you may often encounter unexpected challenges. This book will equip you to navigate these shifts, providing tools to handle uncertain terrain.

Experienced Business Leaders: Even seasoned entrepreneurs face rock-bottom moments. This book serves as your reminder that setbacks are part of the journey, offering fresh perspective on rejuvenating stagnant ventures.

Women Entrepreneurs: Addressing the unique challenges females face in the entrepreneurial realm, this book will empower you to transform your setbacks into stepping stones toward your definition of success. **Diverse Entrepreneurs:** Entrepreneurs from marginalized communities can find strength in stories that reflect their experiences; I will help motivate you to rise above difficulties and make your mark.

Entrepreneurial Innovators: If you are striving to bring innovation to established industries, this book provides insight into forging new paths and embracing failures as opportunities for growth.

Intrapreneurs: For the professional within a larger organization, seeking to create impactful initiatives, you will benefit from the entrepreneurial wisdom shared in this book as it teaches you to pivot and thrive amid challenges.

Consider this book to be a comprehensive toolkit for those of you who dare to dream, create, and innovate, regardless of your stage in the entrepreneurial journey. It's a beacon of hope for when you navigate uncharted waters, providing the guidance needed to turn rock-bottom moments into transformative opportunities for growth and your definition of success.

COUNT YOUR WINS

This book recounts several rock-bottom moments from my life, but I have to admit it wasn't all one big dumpster fire. You see, I learned that after you reach the bottom, you will bounce back. Here are some of the great things that happened when I decided not to give up:

- My first company, Mutt's Sauce, did VIP packages for Adidas, JPMorgan Chase, America's Warrior Partnership, FourBlock, and Bunker Labs, to name a few.

- The United States Playing Card Company created a limited edition deck that honored veteran-run businesses. In the Frontline Leaders deck, Mutt's Sauce is the four of hearts.
- Mutt's Sauce appeared on QVC three times during the coronavirus pandemic.
- I became the co-founder and executive director of a nonprofit, OH Taste Foundation, which is building the 6888 Kitchen Incubator; our team raised $4.3 million in nine months.
- I created a financial literacy course for food businesses that launched in October 2022, and it has over thirty graduates and a huge waiting list.
- I graduated from the Harvard Kennedy School Executive Education program for nonprofit owners.
- I graduated from the Goldman Sachs 10,000 Small Businesses program.
- I've been honored to serve on several boards of directors and trustees, continuing the journey of servant leadership.
- I watched my son thrive even after a terrifying medical event, brought on by COVID-19. He also learned to cook and read by age three.
- I was honored to be named one of the We Are the Mighty's "Mighty 25" top military influencers in the country.
- I was named one of two business owners in Dayton, Ohio to make the inaugural national Bizwomen100 list of women leading in their business communities.

When you believe in something bigger than yourself, *Rock Bottom Has a Trampoline.*

INTRODUCTION

*H*ow *do I get out of here?* This and a million other questions and thoughts raced in my brain. There we were, my husband and I, standing in the foyer on the first floor of our townhouse in Washington, DC in complete silence. *Like two strangers.*

We'd ridden home without exchanging a word, save the couple of times he cursed under his breath, realizing the gravity of the situation.

"Leave my luggage in the garage," I said as I walked past him and up to the second floor to grab my car keys. He stayed downstairs. I paused in front of the door, desperately trying to hide my hand that was shaking with betrayal, disappointment, and regret. *This has happened so many times before: Stay and fight or walk away.* I realized only one of us was making decisions for our future as a couple.

That person was me.

That person, I felt, had always been me.

And I was exhausted.

"Is it true?" I had asked him as soon as we left the restaurant in DC where we were meant to have a romantic dinner. I had just flown back from Ohio where I had given a keynote speech at a business conference. Five minutes before I gave that speech, I received a message from a stranger telling me something that would put an end to my marriage. I basically spent the entire time at dinner staring at the food I was supposed to be eating, while he spent it telling me to just delete the message and block that stranger's phone number.

"Is it true?" I repeated.

Silence.

Silence was the conclusion to our relationship of ten years, five of which we had spent married. "The power couple of the US Air Force," as some of our close friends and colleagues called us. Though we had faced many problems within our marriage and tried to give ourselves credit for "perseverance and growth," this latest one was where I decided to draw the line. This time, there was no trying to patch things up. To me, the ink wasn't even dry on our marriage certificate. None of this seemed real. *We aren't man and wife anymore.*

It was 2017 and I had recently moved in with him to the nation's capital because that's where he was stationed.

"Just move here," he had told me while I was still living in Ohio. "I've got this place all furnished; you don't need to worry about anything."

I did just as he asked: I moved there, bringing nothing more than the clothes I was wearing during the trip, and I didn't worry because he told me he would take care of everything. I moved there as his "military spouse," a title I embraced but that I was somewhat still getting used to, because for the longest time I had also been a fellow military servicemember, and a proud one at that! But I had decided to get out of active duty and settle down with him. So, there I was. In our house—no, erase that. In *his* house, surrounded by *his* furniture, suffering from *his* betrayal.

After I filed for divorce, a judge gave me five days to return to the house and gather my things, with the promise of never returning. "Your husband cannot call, text, or be in a radius of the dwelling."

I stood by the front door asking, "What am I going to do?" to no one, as I hid my face in my hands. No tears came out. I had already spent them all.

I finally opened the door and was immediately assaulted by memories of us. Those memories were sitting on the end table by the couch in the form of a framed wedding photo. They were staring at me in the form of scribbled Post-it

Notes reminding me of upcoming doctors' appointments and conference calls. They were mocking me in the form of a quilt that he bragged about at seemingly every ceremony: "She took sewing classes after work to learn how to patch this quilt from my childhood back together."

Sitting on the kitchen table was an assortment of alcohol (which I had been using a lot to self-medicate) with a note he had written for me. *He really wants me to drink myself to death and forget what I'm here to do.* I kept scanning the house, my heartbeat rising as I remembered not just the memories, but also the arguments, the times I felt like I was living in a bachelor pad, and the hours spent cleaning (cleaning, I learned, is one of my trauma responses; I clean out of stress). My own mother had nicknamed me "Cinderella" because it seemed that every time she asked me what I was doing, I was cleaning the house. "Surely the house isn't always dirty. There're just two of you," she would say. As I stood there, haunted by the ghost of the past, guess what I did? I started cleaning. I removed all traces of myself, save for our giant canvas wedding photo and my wedding dress in the master bedroom closet. Then, I gathered the rest of my belongings, which included a Coleman cot we had bought in case friends or family came to spend the night.

Get out of here, Charlynda, I told myself. But my feet felt as if they were frozen, stuck in that place to which I had dedicated ten years of my life, where I had poured all my hopes and dreams as a young woman. I looked back once again at the house, at my relationship with him, and at my commitment to him. My mother had raised no quitter.

"But she also raised no fool," I said out loud as I walked out that door, forever closing it on the past.

Fast forward a few days, and I was sitting in an empty apartment I had managed to find available for rent. The only furniture in the entire place was my cot, which I had put in the living room. The only thing keeping me company was a bottle of Jack Daniel's. That is, until my phone rang.

I didn't want to answer.

I didn't want to talk to anyone.

But the caller kept insisting, so I gave in.

"Hello?" I said, trying my best not to sound under the effect of alcohol.

"Charlynda, great news!" the female voice on the other end said. I recognized her. She was the editor of a prominent military magazine. "We've decided that we want you to be our cover story."

Oh no . . .

"I'm sorry, what?" I asked, hoping to God that I had misheard.

"We have chosen you to be our featured cover story," she said, her enthusiasm so vivid in her tone that I could almost touch it.

Oh no . . .

She had told me not even a week prior that she had included my story in the list of possible ones that the magazine was going to consider for the cover. At the time I was thrilled, because this magazine is widely distributed across military bases all over the country and even abroad, so it could be great publicity for me and my company.

"We think you represent the new military spouse," she said, her tone growing even more upbeat. "No more the typical wife with the handmade poster waiting at the airport for her servicemember to come home from deployment or the one who has dinner ready every night when he gets off work. Charlynda, you're a powerhouse."

"No, I'm not," I said in thin voice, admitting it to myself as much as her.

"Now, now. Don't be modest," she said, having no idea that the woman she was talking to was completely falling apart. "You are a businesswoman, and a successful one at that!" She had a point. I should have been celebrating. Only ten days prior I had won the grand prize of Bob Evans Farms' grant for veterans, Heroes to CEOs. My wildest dream had even come true: They provided a free mentoring session with *Shark Tank's* Daymond John.

"I know but—"

"You're the owner of Mutt's Sauce, the specialty sauce that represents your grandfather's legacy and that you somehow took from idea to reality, even though you knew nothing about running a small business in the food industry."

She was right again. My grandfather, Charlie "Mutt" Ferrell, Jr., a country boy from Carthage, Tennessee, created this all-purpose sauce in the 1950s. Everybody loved the sauce, and when my grandfather passed away in 2005, we all thought the sauce went with him because he never left us the recipe. Or so we thought. Come to find out, he did leave the recipe—the only recipe—to my mother and instructed her to give it to me when she thought I was ready. I knew I had to do something with this recipe, so I started Mutt's Sauce, the company I had headquartered in Ohio but had been trying to run from Washington, DC so that I could be with my husband. *Ex-husband, now.*

"Are you still there?" the editor asked me, bringing me back to the conversation.

"Ye-yeah," I said, massaging my temples. "Sorry."

"So, what do you say?" she asked. "Are you ready to be on the cover of *Military Spouse* magazine and show our community what it means to be a military spouse in this day and age?"

I sighed. I had to come clean with her, even though I hadn't told anybody about what had happened.

"No, I'm not," I said.

There was a pause. Then she asked, "What do you mean?"

"My life is crumbling around me," I admitted.

"Charlynda, what's going on?" she asked, her sincere concern for me as tangible as her excitement had been just minutes prior.

"I-I . . . I am not a powerhouse. I am a complete failure," I said, and proceeded to recount everything that had happened with my husband and where my life stood as we spoke. "I can't be your cover story. My life is really at rock bottom right now."

"I am so sorry to hear that you've been going through so much pain," she said.

I was about to wish her good day so I could go back to my misery when—

"But I still want you to be on the cover," she said.

What? My mouth went dry.

"But I just said—"

"I know," she interrupted me. "But Charlynda, don't you see? Military spouses have always been seen as dependent upon their military servicemember—heck, they are actually *called* 'dependents.' They are stereotypically portrayed as not being financially independent, their needs and wants always having to come after their servicemember's career, and raising children on their own while dealing with all the issues that come with living on a military base. That's the mold military spouses have been stuck in for decades. You, my dear, are the living and breathing proof that the mold has been not just broken, but completely shattered!"

I had no words.

"You represent the new military spouse," she continued. "The go-getter, the self-sufficient, the entrepreneur, the business savvy, the independent woman. Other military spouses who are out there doing their own thing and succeeding have a need to see themselves represented in the media, because just like you they are rewriting the very definition of the military spouse status quo. Charlynda, this is so much bigger than you."

She's right.

It was in that moment that my mindset shifted. It went from being so stuck on my own situation, my own problems, and my own setbacks to recognizing that I'm part of something that, as the editor said, was much bigger than myself. Yes, personally I felt like I had hit rock bottom. But when I looked around me and understood how my own story played into a much bigger and more important narrative that needed to be conveyed and reinforced, I realized rock bottom has a trampoline.

Being an entrepreneur, chances are you will hit rock bottom over and over again. Success stories make it seem like the road to the top is a straight line, when in reality the road is a constant up and down. It's one heck of a rollercoaster that will test your patience, your faith, your strength, your motivation, and even your purpose. You will be knocked down so hard when you hit rock bottom that you will question whether it's worth getting back up at all, like I did while I was going through my divorce. But, as this book will show you, rock bottom can be many things. Luckily, for every kind of rock bottom there is a trampoline.

Rock bottom is personal, as my own story illustrates. My small business was skyrocketing just as my private life was falling apart, and my personal rock bottom threatened to derail—or worse, completely halt—my professional life. But a personal rock bottom doesn't just entail struggles in your love life. A personal rock bottom can sound like something damaging from within. After I stumbled upon my purpose when I was given my grandfather's recipe, I found myself facing my personal, and very first, rock bottom: my Inner Critic. *You don't know anything about food. You are not qualified to run this business. You should just give the recipe to somebody who can actually do something with it.* These were just a few of the many things I heard the Inner Critic whisper in my head, and I found that it was easy to lean into that voice and just give up. Thankfully, I didn't.

Another kind of rock bottom can resemble hanging out with the wrong crowd. One of the hardest rock bottoms I have ever had to face was when I realized I was surrounded by like-minded people. I thought that if I relied on people who were just as focused as I was on achieving success, my business would flourish. *Wrong!* I put my trust in their hands, and they broke it; I gave them my heart, and they shattered it; I vowed to always do right by them, and they took advantage of me. It was only when I hit rock bottom that I realized like-minded people were not the ones I needed to surround myself with. Rather, I had to be with like-hearted people. (More on this later.)

Rock bottom can also come crashing into your life in the form of loss. I have to admit that at one point I thought, *What is the purpose of launching Mutt's Sauce if my grandfather passed away? He is never going to see what we did with his recipe, so why bother?* Indeed, facing the (sudden) loss of a loved one can be one of the most emotional and challenging rock bottoms any entrepreneur faces in their journey.

Rock bottom can manifest as burnout. Getting a business up and running is no easy feat. It requires mental and physical commitment, long hours of work, great responsibilities, and much more. Entrepreneurship often demands you to always be at and give 100 percent, with very little time or energy left to replenish yourself. As a result, many entrepreneurs experience burnout. Suddenly, you feel like you just have nothing left to give and the only solution seems to be to just quit! But quitting is a permanent decision to a temporary situation.

Rock bottom can also result as a consequence of trauma. At one point or another, your invisible scars are going to remind you that they are still there. "You're disabled? You don't look like it!" people often tell me when they learn I am a disabled veteran. What they assume is that my disability is visible; the reality is, my scars are emotional, mental, and spiritual because of the trauma I have been through while serving in the military. According to the National Council for Behavioral Health, 70 percent of American adults have experienced at least one traumatic event in their life, whether it was during their childhood, while in an adult relationship, because of a natural disaster, or from other circumstances.[1] Therefore, most entrepreneurs will experience a trauma-related rock bottom at some point in their business venture.

Rock bottom can be social. As a Black woman who grew up in the Deep South, I have experienced racism and discrimination in both my personal and professional life. Just like me, seven out of ten Black Americans admit they have experienced discrimination.[2] For people who are neurodiverse, who are part of the LGBTQIA+ community, or who are of a racial minority group, racism and discrimination might be what comes between them and their entrepreneurial dream. Landlords declining to rent an office space to people because of the color of their skin; investors refusing to finance a business because of the owner's sexual orientation; or a company looking down upon a female business owner because of her gender. These are all possible rock bottoms where entrepreneurs could find themselves. A social media post, a comment made during an interview, or even a fashion statement might be offensive to a group of people, and it can turn into the reason why a business venture fails. At the end of the day, rock bottom is defined not just by personal struggles, but also by the social forces and prejudices that can derail even the most determined entrepreneurs.

Another form of social rock bottom is being pushed there through peer pressure. Your colleague wins yet another award and you didn't even win one this year; your friend has a great fitness routine, while yours is nonexistent; your acquaintance has a successful marriage and a picture-perfect family, while yours is falling apart before your very eyes. No matter where

---

1. National Council for Behavioral Health, "How to Manage Trauma," available at: https://www.thenationalcouncil.org/wp-content/uploads/2022/08/Trauma-infographic.pdf.

2. Pew Research Center, "On Views on Race and Inequality, Blacks and Whites Are Worlds Apart," June 27, 2016, available at: https://www.pewresearch.org/social-trends/2016/06/27/5-personal-experiences-with-discrimination/.

you look, your sense of competition is there to remind you that you should do more and be more. Peer pressure can really enhance this sense and throw you off your game—if you spend energy comparing yourself to others and where they are in their journey.

Rock bottom is financial. Perhaps the most common rock bottom among entrepreneurs is not having enough money. You have this great idea but no money to turn it into a reality; you spent the initial funds you had and now have nothing left to move your business forward; the venture is so thrilling and the adrenaline it releases in your body fuels you into action, but it also clouds your mind and judgment so that you spend your money all at once without thinking of the consequences. These are some of the most common scenarios that entrepreneurs find themselves in when it comes to facing the harsh reality of the lack of funds.

However, financial rock bottom can also present itself in the opposite situation: when you have too much money. Believe it or not, having too much money can be just as much of a detriment as is not having enough. When a business venture goes from hopeful idea to highly successful reality, the entrepreneur must be able to think clearly and not fall prey to the dopamine effect. A sudden increase in monetary gains can seduce any entrepreneur into splurging a bit. Maybe you buy that car you've always wanted and now can afford, or take that vacation in the Caribbean you've always dreamed of, or purchase that house in the suburbs you've always wanted to live in. It's hard to resist the urge to spend money and enjoy life. After all, you've worked so hard to get where you are, shouldn't you spoil yourself a little? Remember that with great wealth comes great responsibility. Excessive riches often cause entrepreneurs to lose sight of their goals, demonstrating that too much money can lead to a damaging rock bottom.

Engaging in the wrong partnership can lead to rock bottom as well. History is filled with tales of partnerships gone wrong: John Lennon left The Beatles, Mark Zuckerberg ousted Eduardo Saverin from Facebook ownership, Burt and Lovey Handelsman's divorce crashed their real estate empire, and so forth. This is a rock bottom many entrepreneurs face: getting into business with the wrong person; discovering later that the business partner has a completely different vision of where the business should be heading; and becoming aggravated with the lack of commitment on the business partner's side.

Rock bottom is also making financial decisions you do not want to make. Life happens, and when it does, you might have to make decisions that you are not happy with but that are necessary. You might find yourself in a situation where you must use money you had decided to use for your business for personal reasons. These situations occur when there's a medical bill that was more expensive than you expected, or when you need a last-minute plane ticket home because of a family emergency, or when your car breaks down and you have to replace it. When life happens, you may have to make tough money choices that feel like rock bottom.

But most of all, rock bottom is unpredictable. If you are reading this book, you have more than likely gone through the stock market crashing; the housing market unravel; the terrorist attacks of September 11, 2001; and the pandemic of COVID-19. Clearly, there are certain rock bottoms that cannot be predicted.

Rock Bottom Has a Trampoline will provide you with tangible, helpful methods and solutions to get yourself out of every type of rock bottom you may experience. Chapter by chapter, you will learn how to extract value from adversity, overcome your challenges, and thrive. Most importantly, you'll discover how to turn your rock bottom situation into a trampoline that will propel you toward your definition of entrepreneurial success. Ready? Let's go!

Charlynda Scales
The Like-Hearted™ Mentor

PART I:
ROCK BOTTOM IS PERSONAL

CHAPTER ONE

ROCK BOTTOM IS AN INNER CRITIC

"Your grandfather wanted you to have this," my mother said as she handed me an envelope.

I looked at it and my jaw dropped to the floor.

"Mom," I said in a thin voice. "Is this what I think it is?"

She nodded.

In that envelope, in his own handwriting, was the recipe of my grandfather's sauce. The *secret* recipe, may I add, seeing as he had passed away eight years prior and all of us, including his children and grandchildren, thought that the recipe had died with him and we were therefore condemned to spend life eating food without unique flavor.

"Why give it to me?" I asked, shaking my head in disbelief. "Why now?"

"He told me to give it to Tutti Frutti"—my grandfather's nickname for me—"and he instructed me to do so when I thought you were ready to receive it."

This is crazy. I had called my mother a week prior, lamenting the fact that my lunch could have really used some of my grandfather's sauce. "If only he had left the recipe," I told her. To which she replied, "Come see me in Tennessee."

Though I was stationed at Wright-Patterson Air Force Base in Ohio, as I was active-duty Air Force, I was born and raised in Cookeville, Tennessee. So, there I went to see her as requested, never in a million years imagining that the visit would turn out to be a life-altering one.

"Wait a second," I said, almost jumping at the realization. "What did he say I have to do for the recipe?"

My mother giggled.

"I'm serious," I insisted. "You know he never gave me anything for free. I always had to earn it."

It was true. Throughout my childhood—which I had spent living with my grandparents and my mother—my grandfather, the disciplinarian, always made me work hard for what I wanted.

"Daddy,"—that's how I called him, because he was my only father figure since my own father had moved back to Nigeria, his home country, after what turned out to be a short marriage to my mother—"can I get ten dollars?"

"Tutti Frutti," he would reply. "Get an A on your next test in school and then we can talk about it."

"Daddy, can I get a new bike?"

"Tutti Frutti, help your mother and grandmother with house chores for a month and we'll see."

See what I mean? Every request turned into a negotiation, a transaction. Nothing came for free.

"He didn't say you had to do something to earn it," my mother said. "He just told me to give it to you when I felt you were ready for it."

"And what makes you think I'm ready for it now?" I asked.

"You called me and told me you wished you had the sauce to flavor your food with," she said with a shrug. "Well, now you have the recipe—the *only* recipe. Do something with it."

I looked at the recipe, then back up at her. "Mom, you know I can't cook. What makes you think that I, out of all his nieces, nephews, and grandchildren, are the one who can do something with this recipe? I mean, we even have a professional chef in the family! Why me?"

"Figure it out," she said and walked away.

Figure it out.

I had no idea what I was going to do with the recipe, but I knew I had to do something. For whatever reason, my grandfather had entrusted me, his Tutti Frutti, with his most secret possession, and I did not take that lightly. I knew what that sauce meant to him.

One of five children, and born in 1934, my grandfather earned his nickname "Mutt" thanks to his ability to blend in everywhere and with everyone. He had that type of personality—the magnetic one that attracts people from all walks of life, with different cultural backgrounds, and makes you feel like you belong in his circle, like you have always been good friends even though you've just met him. This personality served him well when, after joining the US Air Force as a teenager, he was sent to Japan during the Vietnam and the Korean Wars. Though his career as an aircraft inspector, and later a crew chief, was demanding, he still managed to always be the life of the party. Every time he had colleagues and friends over at his house, he would host get-togethers and serve his homemade sauce, something he had come up with a few years prior by putting together ingredients he had found in his fridge and combining them to form a sweet, tangy, and slightly spicy sauce.

The more parties he hosted, the more people got to know about the sauce. And let me tell you something about that sauce: Mutt's Sauce was so much more than just barbecue. It was an experience. Every time the sauce was present on the dining table, there was laughter all around, friendship, smiles, good times, hopes, and dreams. And of course, great food. That sauce had the power of bringing people together, of making them forget that they were in a different country and could have been called at any given moment to go fight in a war that had been claiming thousands upon thousands of innocent lives. Mutt's Sauce was able to erase social status, race, gender, religious beliefs, and everything else people use to highlight differences among cultures. That sauce was so delicious that its flavor could be appreciated in every language, whether it be English, Korean, Japanese, or any other one. That sauce united people as human beings, not as American or Japanese, not as Black or White, not as enlisted or officer, and not as Muslim or Christian.

"Mutt, you should bottle this up and sell it," people would tell him.

"Yeah, yeah," he would say, waving them away as if dismissing them.

Over the years, I have wondered why he never did bottle it up and sell it, or why he never shared the recipe with anybody. There were countless people who asked, pleaded, begged, and even tried to bribe him for that recipe. But my grandfather's lips were sealed. So, you can understand why years later as I stood in the kitchen of my mother's house in Tennessee, holding that recipe in my hands, I felt like I had just been entrusted with the Holy Grail.

Figure it out.

Call it cliché, but after talking to Mom, I had a dream about a little country store at the top of the hill from where my grandparents lived when I was a child. My granddad used to ask me to fetch stuff from that corner store, often sending me there with a list handwritten on a paper bag or spare piece of paper and a couple dollars. Even as a child, they never checked my ID for the items I fetched. In this dream, however, every shelf had an identical bottle on it. My grandfather's face was on every bottle. It was such a wild dream, that I woke up shaking my head, as if to shake out a crazy thought.

Once I was back in Ohio, self-doubt began sinking its sharp talons deep into my consciousness.

I know nothing about cooking. "She can't even boil water!" I clearly recall my cousins teasing. God had gifted me with a lot, but the ability to cook was not one of them. How could I possibly turn a recipe into a successful business if I could barely follow it myself?

I know nothing about the food industry. Again, true. I had graduated with a degree in aerospace science and business management and held an MBA in strategic leadership. None of the classes I took had taught me how to turn a handwritten recipe from 1956 into a bottled sauce that people could buy.

I am on active duty, I can't run a business while serving my country. Being in the military is a full-time job like no other. Of course, you work your shift and then you can go home and rest, but the truth is, if something comes up, if something happens, you have to get back to work right away. There can be no, "Sorry, I'm busy with this farmer's market today. I can't come in." The military must always come first, even before family sometimes. "Service before self" is one of the things that the military requires of you. When I signed up to become an Air Force officer, I understood the commitment I was making because I had seen my uncles, cousins, and grandfather make it before me.

I can't do it.

I am not the right person.

That voice in my head got louder and louder every single day. The more I heard it, the more I believed it. The more I believed it, the more I wanted to hide that recipe someplace safe and pretend like it had never been given to me.

If I try and fail, it's going to be such a disappointment for me, my mother, and my entire family . . . It's not an if. I am going to fail.

There it was. Rock bottom.

This rock bottom had a voice that I had allowed to grow stronger. This rock bottom had not been caused by anybody around me. This rock bottom had come straight from within me. This rock bottom had a first and last name: Inner Critic.

I was at a crossroad: Try to do something with this recipe or keep living like it didn't exist?

Then, I remembered something. It was the day I commissioned into the US Air Force. My grandfather, battling stage 4 lung cancer that had metastasized all over his body, holding his walking cane to keep himself upright, came to me and said: *"Congratulations, Tutti Frutti."* Then, he gave me the Silver Dollar Salute.[3] I had tears in my eyes for how special that moment was to me. What an honor to be saluted by my grandfather, who passed away shortly after.

He had raised me, supported me in ways I couldn't understand as a child but that I had come to appreciate as an adult. He had instilled in me important values: Love your family and work hard. He had been there for me since before I was even born. He gave me the recipe, which meant he trusted me to do the right thing with it. Though he hadn't left instructions on what he wanted me to do with it, I believed it should be shared with others. I didn't yet know how, but I realized that my grandfather knew something my mother felt as well: I was going to figure it out.

That's when I decided which route I was going to choose at that intersection. But I could not do it alone for one simple

---

3. "A revered tradition in the U.S. armed forces that dates back to the 19th century. The coin presentation is a token of appreciation for the enlisted member's guidance and mentoring. The coin recipient will then follow the military career of the newly-commissioned officer." Team, Lcc Writing. "Silver Dollar Salute Ceremony - Littleton Coin Blog." Littleton Coin Company Blog, October 21, 2022, https://blog.littletoncoin.com/silver-dollar-salute/.

reason: I had no idea where to even begin. And that's when I knew I had to turn to people who could guide me through the process of turning a piece of paper into a business plan.

I still remember the day I met my SCORE mentor.[4] A man the same age my grandfather would have been had he still been alive, John Soutar listened carefully while I explained what Mutt's Sauce was and how the recipe had ended up with me. After I was done with my longwinded monologue, which had been interspersed with, "I don't know what to do. I feel like I won't be able to do it," he sighed heavily, leaned back in his chair, and said: "What I hear is that your grandfather cared a great deal about his family and he wanted to do right by them. There was a lot he wanted to do for you all."

He gets it.

"He just ran out of time," he said.

I nodded, looking down at my hands sitting on the table, my fingers interlaced as if I was praying.

"But he has you," he said.

I looked up at him and saw a hint of a smile on his face, which I mirrored.

"I don't think you just have a couple of bottles in that recipe," he added. "I see this on the shelves of grocery stores, for example." He explained his vision for my product and listed so many ideas that seemed so out of reach for me at the time. "What, you don't believe it can be done?" he asked, probably noticing the question mark that had formed on my face.

"I . . . I am on active duty, and this sounds like it's going to require a lot of my time, which I might not have," I said.

"Nah," he said. "Like a good little soldier, you are going to follow a checklist that I'm going to give you. All you have to do is commit an hour of your day to this list. One step at a

---

4. SCORE is a community of mentors who volunteer to help guide businessowners through the hardships of entrepreneurship, https://www.score.org/.

time." Then he leaned forward and said almost in a whisper, "You can do this."

I can do this?

He believed in my grandfather's vision, in what the recipe could turn into, and in me. He was willing to guide me through every step I had to take to turn this paper into a business. I wasn't alone in this. I had his mentorship and the theory of what he called the "speed of determination." "However determined you are to make this happen is how fast this will happen," he said.

I can do this.

Evening after evening, no matter how tired I was from work, I would sit at my desk and work on one item on that checklist. Slowly but surely, I went through every item. File for my business license—check. Find a manufacturer—check. Find someone to design a logo and label—check. Get nutritional values listed (heck, get the product tested in a laboratory)—check, and so forth. Four months later, I had a product line that I could sell. Mutt's Sauce had two flavors: Original and Sweet N Spicy. Sweet N Spicy was based off the original recipe. I had a capsaicin allergy and could never eat foods with pepper. My grandfather had made a version for me without pepper, which I named "Original" as an inside joke with my family.

I can do this!

"Now that you have the physical product, you can begin selling it on the weekends," my mentor said after I showed up with the completed checklist. "Go to farmer's markets and local festivals, and visit mom-and-pop stores to introduce yourself and Mutt's Sauce. Then, during the week, you are an Air Force officer and do what you have to do, but in the evening, you have to keep up with the business paperwork."

Once again, I did just as he suggested, and Mutt's Sauce kept growing. That is not to say that Inner Critic—also known as Imposter Syndrome—left. On the contrary, he set up camp inside of me and kept talking to me (at times he whispered while other times he screamed so loud I couldn't hear anything else around me). I don't believe Inner Critic will ever go away, but neither will my motivation and perseverance.

SECRET SAUCE: How can entrepreneurs turn the rock bottom of Inner Critic into a trampoline?

Remember that you don't have to feel qualified to be qualified. Don't let the Inner Critic's voice stay inside of you. Don't try to suppress it, as it won't go away. Rather, sit down with it and listen to what it has to say. Then, turn to people who support you and are trustworthy and let them know what your questions are and what doubts you are having. Allow yourself to listen to what they have to say and believe in their words of encouragement. You will soon realize that their voices will tune out the Inner Critic, thus leaving room for you to focus on your purpose and mission.

Refocus your mindset. Dwelling on anxieties saps energy. Instead, visualize desired outcomes and plan constructive actions to achieve them. If your mind tends to just run away from your control until you finally find it deep down into the rabbit hole of what-ifs, try using effective visualization by creating a vision board. Gather supplies like a poster board, a notebook, magazines, photos, and colorful pens or markers. Then, start writing down what your goals are, what you aspire to be and become, and where you wish your business to be in the future. Cut out photos that inspire you, snippets from articles, or motivational quotes. Glue them all together on the poster board in a way that feels good to you and ta-da! When you feel like you need to refocus your mindset but are having a hard time doing so, look back at your vision board. It will help you stay the course without losing sight of what you're working toward.

Be your cheerleader and give yourself some grace. Celebrate small wins and give yourself credit for showing up despite your self-doubts. Developing a supportive inner voice weakens the Inner Critic. Don't worry about the naysayers, they're not the ones living your life. Keep working toward your goals and, if you need a little extra motivation to do so, don't forget to set a reward for yourself at the end of a task that can motivate you to push through the hard times, the tight deadlines, the endless paperwork, and the umpteenth meeting of the week.

Don't take it personally and stop overthinking. The Inner Critic attacks your work, not your worth. Letting its harshness reflect on your identity gives it too much power. Your situation is not your identity. The more time you spend thinking, the less time you're spending on the action of bouncing back. The quote "perfection is procrastination in disguise" holds great truth. Accept constructive criticism and use the suggestions in a way that will work for you and your business.

You don't have to feel qualified to be qualified. The rock bottom of self-doubt may feel inescapable, but you have more control than you think. Disarm the Inner Critic and use your energy to propel yourself to greater heights.

CHAPTER TWO

ROCK BOTTOM IS THE WRONG CROWD

"I f you want someone who's agreeable, then she's not the right candidate," he said.

I didn't know what to reply. All I wanted was to hire an executive assistant who could help me run Mutt's Sauce in Ohio while I was trying to not completely fall apart back in Washington, DC, during my divorce. I had never even met the woman, but I knew her husband—a fellow military member. But the way he was describing her to me didn't make much sense.

She had come highly recommended, I thought to myself, while wondering why her husband wasn't singing her praise.

"What do you mean?" I asked him.

"I mean, she shares the same values as you, but you'll be shocked because she'll rarely agree with you," he said. "So, if you want a 'Yes ma'am' type of assistant, don't waste your time in hiring her. But if you want someone who will advise you from a place of love, then she's your girl."

Advise me from a place of love, I heard his voice echo in my head. It felt just like what I needed. With my entire life falling apart all around me—the divorce had made a mess of just about everything—I could have really used advice from a place of love.

"When can I meet her?" I asked him.

"Whenever you have time," he said.

So, I got on a plane as soon as I could and flew back to Ohio to meet her. After the classic small talk to break the ice, I went straight to the point: "I want you to know the whole truth before you get yourself into this situation," I said thinly, because I was about to hear myself voice words that I had kept secret from everybody else who wasn't my immediate family. "I am going through possibly the hardest time in my life." I told her everything in what felt like one single breath. She learned of my new marital status, my empty apartment, and my fears of running Mutt's Sauce while in a different state.

"I have heard so much about you," she said. "And I love everything I heard about you."

Here comes the but . . .

"From what you've just told me, I can see that we share some of the same values and that our hearts are in the same place," she added.

I was still waiting for the but.

She took a deep breath, and I braced for impact.

"And that's good enough for me." She shrugged.

Then, silence.

There was no but?

I waited a few more seconds.

There was no *but.*

"So you're in?" I asked just to be sure she wanted to accept the position.

"Of course; just give me a couple of weeks to go over the paperwork and evaluate where we're at as a company," she said in such a tone that made it clear to me that declining the job offer had never crossed her mind.

I flew back to DC knowing that my business was in good hands. But I couldn't possibly have known that on our next call, she would tell me I had to let go of more than half my staff.

"But why?" I asked her.

"Because you have to save money," she said. "You're paying thousands of dollars in rent for an empty apartment, plus your divorce lawyer, plus everything else you've got going on that is taking money out of your account as if it were chilled water on a hot day. Your business is not making enough at the moment to sustain itself. So, unless you plan on somehow winning the lottery real quick, you need to cut contracts."

"But they are good friends of mine," I pleaded with her. "I can't let them go, they said they were going to help me expand my business."

"I get it they're your buddies," she said, unmovable. "But what they're charging you to keep them around is too much. And where are the results of what they said they were going to do? The real problem here is that you're not surrounding yourself with people who care about you the way family does, but rather with people who just think like you. That's not enough when it comes to being successful."

Her words made sense to me, and something inside of me told me I could trust her, even if I had only known her for two weeks. I think the reason why I decided to follow her advice was because she told me that she cared about me and Mutt's Sauce. And I believed that she cared, or she wouldn't have been having such a hard conversation with me.

"So what should I do now?" I asked her.

"Aside from cutting back on more than half of the contracts you have in place, I think you should move back to Ohio."

"What?" I said, "I can't do that."

"Really? Why not?"

"Well, I just started this new job at the Federal Aviation Administration (FAA). They basically created the position for me. I can't let them down by quitting a few days after starting. I can't do that to my boss, who is excellence personified."

"Alright, just my two cents," she said.

Needless to say, I followed her advice on the contracts and cut back in a major way. But I wasn't ready to follow her advice about moving back to Ohio. At least, not until the universe worked whatever force it needed to and basically made it happen.

It was like the perfect storm. Though I had been extremely grateful for the job at the FAA, I wasn't performing up to par because of all the chaos around me. The nastiness of the divorce had escaped the confounds of my home and branched out into every aspect of my life, no matter how hard I tried to keep that mess under control. Because of the emotional state I was in, I would bring eyedrops with me to work every day just so people wouldn't notice that I had been secretly crying in the bathroom. One day, I missed a meeting because I was in the bathroom crying, and a few minutes after I got out, I saw Fawn Freeman, my boss, with her arms crossed. She looked at me with her icy blue eyes that perfectly fit her platinum blonde hair, and said, "Come to my office, we need to talk."

Uh-oh. I had never been in trouble with her before and I didn't want to ever disappoint her. She had this Goldie Hawn personality, a magnetic one, the kind you just want to be around. But when it came down to business, people stopped talking whenever she walked into a room because they knew and respected the position she held.

I swallowed a painful gulp of air while sitting down at her desk, waiting for her to initiate whatever conversation she wanted to have with me.

"How are you?" she said, sitting in front of me, the door to her office now closed to give us privacy.

"I'm doing well," I replied in the most automated way I knew how. That was the prepackaged answer I had been giving people as of lately. Well, actually, all my life. One of the many things my grandfather taught me was to never cry in front of people. Or cry in general. Stoicism is where our strength was, I learned. Take the hit, learn from it, and move on.

But Fawn saw right through me. She leaned forward and whispered, "Don't you ever lie to me."

"Ma'am?" I swallowed another painful gulp of air.

"You're not fine," she said. "You haven't been fine for quite some time."

She's been watching me.

"You understand this is a very important position, one for which I have handpicked you out of the Pentagon to come work with me. Your performance, as of the last few weeks, has not been where it needs to be. So, what's going on?"

Time for the truth.

But words wouldn't come out.

What came out, instead, was something totally unexpected: tears. So many tears. I completely broke down in her office.

And she did the most incredible thing: She got up, walked over to me, and hugged me. I'm not talking about a quick hug. No, she held on to me because in that moment job titles didn't matter, roles didn't matter, and work etiquette didn't matter. It was sisterhood. One woman letting another woman clearly in distress, know that "Hey, I got you." That hug felt like an, "I've been there" hug.

After I finally calmed down, I explained to her everything that had been going on with me. She listened throughout, and when I was done talking, she asked me: "What is the right thing to do for your life?"

I was about to answer, but she stopped me as if able to read my mind.

"Forget this job." Then, she repeated: "What is the right thing to do for your life?"

I took a deep breath and said, "Well, my assistant says I should move back to Ohio."

I laughed it off because I didn't want Fawn to take this as my way of saying, *I'm jumping ship*.

But she saw right through me, yet again. "Maybe this is exactly what you should do."

Our conversation that day ended with a promise on my part that I would think about it. And I did think about it. But the more I thought about it, the more questions came up: Where am I going to stay in Ohio? Am I really ready to leave DC, the place I had moved to for love? DC had promised me so much: life as a military spouse, a high-powered career, and a beautiful place to stay with my husband. Instead, it had delivered the most painful reality check.

I had hit rock bottom.

I had moved to DC to be around like-minded people, who then ended up breaking my heart. I had trusted my business to be in the hands of like-minded people who didn't take it where they promised they would and almost made it go belly up.

Clearly, surrounding myself with like-minded people had not been the right thing to do. Though it was so easy to do because I saw eye-to-eye and really got along with them. If I suggested something, the response was always, "Let's do it!" If I answered a question, I always provided the right answer. And it felt great to be right all the time, it boosted my ego, which blinded my vision. I could no longer see that keeping these people around me was starting to rot my world. Until a like-hearted person showed up at my apartment in Washington, DC with a U-Haul truck after learning that I had left my job at FAA and had extensive foot surgery. That person was my executive assistant.

"What are you doing here?" I asked her, blinking in disbelief, while I tried to balance myself on crutches.

"I'm helping you move back to Ohio," she said, entering my apartment with purpose as if she was ready to start packing up.

"I don't need help with the move," I said, limping toward her.

She turned around, raised an eyebrow, and said, "Get over yourself."

That didn't feel nice to my ego. But I took it because she was right. It was time for me to not only get over it, but to also check my ego at the door. Box after box, she packed up all my stuff and put it in the truck.

"I don't have anywhere to stay," I said in a whisper, mortified of my own admission, as I sat in the passenger seat.

"I know," she said, "that's why I've already told my husband you're staying with us until you find your own place." Then, she drove us out of that city that had represented so many high highs and low lows for me and straight to Ohio, back to my business and myself.

As I saw the lights of DC fade away in the rearview mirror, I couldn't help but think of the two women who had made it possible for me to start over—the one at the wheel and Fawn, who had given me a glowing recommendation that allowed me to secure my next job. These were my like-hearted people, the ones who did what was necessary because they cared, not because they just wanted to boost my ego.

They were the trampoline in my rock bottom.

SECRET SAUCE: How can entrepreneurs surround themselves with like-hearted people instead of like-minded people?

Check your ego at the door. That's the most important step, or you'll never be receptive to constructive criticism, and therefore, growth. As my story showed, the like-minded people I surrounded myself with did nothing but boost my ego and crash my life. The like-hearted people, on the other hand, gave me a reality check and forced me to be honest with myself and be humble about where I was in my life at the time. That's when real growth happened.

In the entrepreneurship journey, one often seeks camaraderie and support from individuals with similar aspirations and perspectives. However, a crucial shift needs to occur—from surrounding oneself with like-minded people to embracing relationships with like-hearted individuals. This transformative approach is underpinned by a critical principle: checking your ego at the door.

Ego checking is the foundation of growth. Start by acknowledging that your ego can be a stumbling block or a stepping stone to your growth. Successful entrepreneurs recognize that unchecked ego can hinder personal and professional development. Therefore, setting aside your ego allows you to open yourself to constructive criticism and new perspectives, essential for progress.

Move from a like-minded to a like-hearted crowd. While surrounding yourself with like-minded individuals might create a comfort zone, it often results in an echo chamber that shields you from critical feedback. Instead, focus on building connections with like-hearted people. These individuals will identify with your values, passions, and aspirations, creating a foundation for deep and meaningful relationships.

Embrace constructive criticism. Like-hearted people are more likely to provide you with honest feedback, even if it's uncomfortable. Their genuine care for your well-being and growth drives them to share insights that promote self-awareness and improvement. Embrace their constructive criticism as a gift that fuels your evolution as an entrepreneur. The military mantra, "Please, sir or ma'am, may I have another?" makes me giggle at how accurate it is. It is typically said while doing physical training, like pushups, and you're in so much pain, but you ask the training instructor to give you more pain. Progress isn't always painless.

Embrace reality and humility. My grandfather and I used to enjoy walking through the grassy fields surrounding the house in Cookeville. He would share his memories of Korea and Vietnam, which often sounded like tall tales. One day, he told me something that made no sense to me at the age of six, but it now is crystal clear: "Tutti Frutti, humility will take you farther than money." Humility is the opposite of being egotistical. It's rooted in a sense of gratitude, in the understanding that the world does not revolve around you but that you are a part of it. I've been seen on stages, speaking with people who had way more money and influence than I have. How'd I get there? I expressed being grateful for the opportunity and focused on giving more than I took. Success is a journey riddled with ups and downs, but your humility can become a cornerstone for actual progress.

Cultivate honesty with yourself. Surrounding yourself with like-hearted people encourages authenticity. If you've ever been around someone with narcissistic personality disorder, the first thing you notice is how much and how adept they are at lying. They are very convincing because they've already mastered lying to one person—themselves. They deeply believe the outrageous lies they tell themselves. The same is true for you. Whatever you tell yourself, you will believe. Henry Ford famously said, "Whether you believe you can or can't, you're right." You're doing better than you may be telling yourself. The situation you're in may not be as bad as you think. Your ability to lead and make an impact even if you've screwed up in the past is still valid; people need to hear that you screwed up and then learned your lesson and recovered.

Nurture mutual growth. Like-hearted relationships foster a two-way street of growth. As you receive guidance and support, reciprocate by offering the same to others. Engage in meaningful discussions, share experiences, and challenge each other to step outside your comfort zones. This reciprocity amplifies the benefits of the relationship.

Create a diverse network. Like-hearted individuals can come from diverse backgrounds and industries. By connecting with a range of people who share your core values but offer different perspectives, you enrich your understanding of the world and expand your problem-solving toolkit.

Foster a supportive ecosystem. Cultivate an ecosystem of like-hearted connections that extends beyond immediate colleagues and peers. Seek mentors, advisors, and friends who genuinely care about your success and well-being. This web of relationships creates a safety net during challenging times.

Remember, your entrepreneurial journey is not just about achieving financial success but also about personal growth and fulfillment. Surrounding yourself with like-hearted individuals who challenge, support, and inspire you can be the catalyst for transformative change, both in your business endeavors and your character. So, check your ego at the door, embrace the power of like-hearted connections, and watch as your entrepreneurial path becomes a remarkable voyage of growth and discovery.

CHAPTER THREE

ROCK BOTTOM IS SUFFERING A LOSS

"You were the one who wanted to come to the Black Enterprise Entrepreneur Conference," RoShawn, the young man who had designed the Mutt's Sauce logo, said. "So why are we in this bar now ordering drinks?"

Because I want to drown my sorrows in alcohol, I wanted to say. But what actually came out of my mouth was, "Well, what's the point in staying at the conference? I wanted to go there because they had a pitch contest, and if I was chosen to pitch my business, then I might have had a chance to get people to invest in my company. But I wasn't chosen to pitch, so I don't need to stay there. Now, let's focus on more important things: What are you drinking?"

He looked at me with a raised eyebrow. "Nothing."

"Suit yourself," I said and turned toward the barman to catch his attention.

Just as I was about to place my order, RoShawn said, "We should go back and listen to other people's pitches. I'm sure there's a lot we could learn from them."

I looked at him and—

"What can I get you started with?" the bartender asked me.

"Oh," I said, looking at him, then back at RoShawn, then back at him. I had a decision to make here: cry on myself while drinking or put my bruised ego aside and go learn something from the people who were chosen to give the pitch. "Nothing, thank you." I said and stood up. I glanced at RoShawn and nodded my head toward the door. We were going back to the conference.

We had barely made it inside the room when a woman, whom I recognized as being one of the conference organizers, approached me in a hurry. "Oh, there you are. Quick, get on stage. The first five companies to physically get on that stage are going to pitch to investors!"

"Wait, what?" I was confused.

"You have sixty seconds to pitch it," she said in a loud tone. "Go, go!"

Honestly, the rest is a blur. I know I rushed to the stage, I know I said something but was interrupted by the buzzer (I had prepared a five-minute pitch, not a one-minute pitch), and I know that a woman on the judging panel called me to her when I got off the stage.

"My name is Jacqueline Neal and I used to sit on the board for Heinz and Kraft," she said. "You're in the wrong room."

"I'm in the wrong room?" I was even more confused than when I was told to rush on stage.

"*Shark Tank* is in the building right now, did you know that?"

My jaw dropped.

"The producers are down the hall. There's a lady handing out bracelets, but I think she's about to leave. If you hurry, you could still catch her and get in line to pitch them."

I couldn't believe it. I thanked her, parted ways with RoShawn who wanted to stay and keep listening to other people pitching, and I rushed down the hall to look for the lady.

"Ma'am, please wait!" I yelled when I saw a woman holding a whole bunch of bracelets. She was just about to open the door and leave the building. "I need a bracelet!"

She turned around and said, "Alright, but you're number 500. Basically, you're going to be standing in the line for the rest of the day. You still want a bracelet?"

"Yes ma'am," I said.

"Alright," she said, handing me the bracelet. "You'll have sixty seconds to pitch the producers. Just be sure to tell them why you should be on *Shark Tank*."

"Thank you," I said and made my way to the line. Hours went by and I stood there patiently—but anxiously—waiting for my turn to arrive.

Finally, number 500 was called. It was my turn. I walked into the room, stood in front of the producers, and made my pitch.

"How long have you been in business?" one of them asked after I was done.

"Six months," I said.

"And you've made how much from sales?"

"A little over $30,000."

"In six months?" another one asked.

"Yes, sir," I said.

"Are you in big stores?" the other one replied.

"No, I'm only in a couple of mom-and-pop stores," I said.

"So you're only in mom-and-pop stores, you haven't even been in business for a year, and you've sold $30,000 worth of sauce?"

"Yes sir," I said.

"And what do you do for a living?" he asked.

"I'm an active duty military officer," I said.

They were silent for a second and I didn't know why.

"Would you like to try Mutt's Sauce?" I offered.

"We're not allowed to try the food," one of them replied. Then he cleared his voice and said, "Listen, someone will be in touch with you, possibly, if we think you're good to proceed to the next round."

That was my cue to thank them for their time and leave the room for another hopeful business owner.

A couple of days later, my phone rang.

"Hi Charlynda, I'm calling to tell you that the producers you pitched to for *Shark Tank* were so impressed and you've made it to the next round!" a young, bubbly woman said.

I could have jumped up and down with joy when I got that call. I couldn't believe it!

"Thank you, that's great news!" I tried to play it cool. "So, what do I do now?"

She went on to explain that I would be pitching again and with every successful pitch, I would be getting one step closer to going to Hollywood and being on the show. She told me how to pitch to them via video and what time, and I showed up. Successful pitch after successful pitch, I eventually got the call of a lifetime.

"You're going to Hollywood!" she said. "And you're leaving tomorrow."

Thank goodness my military colleagues—most of them, anyway—had been incredibly supportive of me through these past few months (my first pitch for the show was in May 2014 and this was September of the same year), as I kept having to take time off to go and make updated pitch videos. This time, being such short notice, they really stepped up to make it possible for me to get on a plane and go from Ohio to California within less than twenty-four hours.

"Make us proud," one of them said. "First active-duty Air Force service member to be on the show!"

It was true. There had never been one before, and I couldn't have been more honored to be the first.

On the day of the show, I learned that the one shark I was really hoping to pitch wasn't going to be there: Daymond John. Though I highly respected the other Sharks, I felt like my values and vision aligned with Daymond John the most, as we had quite a bit in common: We were both raised by single mothers, we placed family above all, and we weren't afraid to work hard for our dreams. But that wasn't the only obstacle I faced that day. I also learned that I had to cook as part of my pitch.

"How am I going to cook if I'm in a hotel room?" I wondered out loud. Thankfully, the hotel was kind enough to let me use their refrigerator to stock the fresh food I had to go out and buy at the last minute: salmon and fruit. I pitched Mutt's Sauce as being the perfect condiment for every meal, so I had to prove to the Sharks that it could be used on a main as well as a side dish.

Eventually, having overcome obstacle after obstacle, my chance to appear before the sharks came. The famous double doors slid open and there they were, sitting right in front of me. I took a deep breath and made my presentation.

"You said that Mutt's Sauce is a year-round condiment, right?" one of them asked when the time for questions came.

"Yes," I said, as confident as possible.

"But you've only been in business for six months, so how can you prove that it can be used year-round?"

Uh-oh, what do I tell them now?

"Well, though I can't prove it to you in an official way, Mutt's Sauce has been around since the early 1950s, when my grandfather first came up with the recipe, so I can tell you that it's lasted the test of time," I said, trying to save the moment.

"Do you have any other obligations besides this?" another shark asked.

"Yes," I replied, trying to conceal my actual job. Why? The Air Force had asked me to memorize official talking points related to my position in the military, and the number one rule was: Don't quit your job on national TV because the military and serving are your highest priority. *That answer will not sit well with the Sharks who want me to be all in,* I thought.

Cue Kevin O'Leary, aka. Mr. Wonderful. He asked the question so directly that it was jarring. "What the heck do you do that's more important than scaling this company?"

Oh man . . . how do I answer this one? Though I couldn't reveal it on national television, I had been thinking about leaving active duty.

"At this time, I cannot focus exclusively on Mutt's Sauce because of my contractual obligations with the US Air Force," I admitted. Instantly, I could see their body language change. Of course they weren't going to say serving isn't as important as Mutt's Sauce. This deal was dead and I could see it on their faces.

In the end, I did not receive an offer of investment from any one of them.

To say I was devastated would be an understatement. I felt like I had let so many people down, from all my colleagues who took on my shifts to allow me to travel and pitch for the show to my family.

That's when I hit rock bottom. *I disappointed my family.* They say that an entrepreneur is someone who jumps off a cliff and learns to build a parachute during the fall. I find that to be true, but only in part. I hadn't jumped; I had been pushed off the cliff. When my mother gave me the recipe my grandfather had left her, with the specific instructions of giving it to Tutti Frutti when I was ready, I was re-evaluating my life. *Should I leave the military? Should I move to the nation's capital? Should I become a full-time military spouse?* My partner and I had been dating so long, we might as well have been common-law married at that point. I had simply been in a holding pattern in several aspects of my life. But then, my mother gave me the recipe and—push! Off the entrepreneurial cliff I went.

Not only was I falling, but this huge loss on *Shark Tank* made me feel as though I couldn't even build my own parachute. As I flew back to Ohio, I kept thinking: *Why am I doing this?* My grandfather, the inventor of Mutt's Sauce, had passed away. He was never going to witness anything of what I was attempting to build as I tirelessly worked day and night to make the business a success. He was never going to pat me on the shoulder and tell me I did a good job. He was never going to come with me to a farmers' market and proudly smile with every bottle we sold. He was never going to see how many people across the country (and eventually abroad) were gathering around the dining table and share stories as they enjoyed food made even more special by his sauce.

That realization almost brought me to a complete halt. But then I remembered the speech I gave on *Shark Tank* and how everyone who worked on that show had learned about my grandfather's story. That's when I realized that though Mutt himself wasn't there to witness his sauce's success, I had the opportunity to talk about him every time I sold a bottle. Every time someone asked me why the name Mutt's Sauce or who was the man pictured in the logo (in case you haven't noticed, my grandfather's face *is* the logo), I had the chance to share his story and keep him alive through storytelling. Eventually, his face even ended up in an official deck of Bicycle cards because they released a special edition honoring small businesses.

Though I moved past the *Why am I doing this?* part, I wanted to understand why I felt the need to ask myself that question to begin with and why the *Shark Tank* loss almost brought me to close down the business. The answer came after some serious self-reflection: I needed validation. You see, ever since I can remember, I always wanted my grandfather to be proud of me: Whenever I got a good grade in school, he was the first person I told because I wanted and needed his validation. When I decided to join the military, I wanted and needed him to tell me it was the right decision. When I launched Mutt's Sauce, I wanted and needed him to tell me I was doing it right. But because he wasn't there to give me that validation, I suddenly found myself seeking it from other people. And when it didn't come, I felt even more lost until I understood that I had been looking for validation in all the wrong places. The only person I needed that validation from was someone who should have given it to me the entire time but for some reason didn't think she was worthy enough of it: myself.

Throughout my career as an entrepreneur, I have met so many other business owners seeking that validation from an outside source. Perhaps it was the woman whose former partner told her she would never be anything without him; perhaps it was a man who grew up with an absent father; or perhaps it was that person who had so many odds stacked up against them. Each one of them turned their pain into fuel and used it to jump off that cliff. But, just as it happened to me, while they were busy building their parachute, they asked themselves: *Why am I doing this?* That former partner was long gone, the absent father was never going to come back, and the odds were still making it so much more difficult to become successful.

Then, it happened: The woman realized that she didn't need her ex-partner's validation to be and feel successful; the man didn't need to shove it in his father's face that he made it even without him; and that person looked at the odds and realized they could use them to build the parachute that was going to save their life. Their validation came from where it matters the most: from within.

SECRET SAUCE: How can entrepreneurs stop seeking validation from outside sources?

This is a journey about self-discovery and self-actualization. You might not realize that, on some level, you're still trying to please someone whose opinion no longer matters or who's not in your life anymore. The loss might have been familial, or maybe it was the end of a relationship that you're now grieving, or it was a resounding *no* from potential investors. But you have to keep on pushing forward because on the other side of loss and pain resides self-actualization. And that's where you will finally realize that you're exactly where you're meant to be and who you're meant to be.

Life has a peculiar way of humbling even the most resolute entrepreneurs. Loss is an inevitable companion on this tumultuous journey. It might manifest as a failed venture, a shattered partnership, or a market downturn that threatens your dreams. At rock bottom, the pain of loss is palpable, but within it lies the seed of resilience and growth. Here are some helpful insights for when you're navigating the rock bottom of loss.

Allow yourself to grieve. When faced with a significant loss, it's important to give yourself permission to grieve. The emotions you feel are valid and processing them is a crucial step toward healing and moving forward. Suppressing your emotions can hinder your ability to learn and grow from the experience.

Extract lessons from failure. Every setback, no matter how painful, carries valuable lessons. Reflect on what went wrong, what factors contributed to the loss, and how you could have approached things differently. This self-assessment can lead to insights that shape your future decisions and strategies. If you think it could be beneficial to you, write down the steps you took and analyze the ones that led you to the loss. Seeing the steps written black on white can help you visualize them better, which will then help you avoid them after you dust yourself off and try again.

Cultivate resilience. Resilience is born out of adversity. Embracing loss as a part of your journey helps you build a robust mindset that can withstand future challenges. Resilience isn't about avoiding failure; it's about bouncing back stronger and wiser each time.

Re-evaluate your goals and priorities. Loss often prompts a reassessment of your goals and priorities. Take this opportunity to reflect on whether your objectives align with your passions and values. Adjust your course if needed, ensuring your endeavors are in harmony with your authentic self.

Lean on your support system. Surround yourself with your like-hearted connections during times of loss. Share your experiences and feelings with them, as they can offer empathy, insights, and even their own stories of overcoming adversity. A strong support system can help alleviate the isolation that often accompanies loss.

Innovate and adapt. Loss can be a catalyst for innovation and adaptation. As you navigate through setbacks, challenge yourself to find creative solutions and pivot when necessary. Adapting to changing circumstances is a hallmark of successful entrepreneurship.

Focus on what you can control. Loss can make you feel powerless, but focusing on what you can control empowers you to take proactive steps. Direct your energy toward aspects within your sphere of influence, whether by refining your skills, optimizing your processes, or building new relationships.

CHAPTER FOUR

ROCK BOTTOM IS BURNOUT

"Have you been running a marathon?" the doctor in the emergency room asked me as he monitored my heart rate.

"No sir," I said, shivering with fear on the hospital bed. "My heart just started racing like this and I got scared that something was seriously wrong with me, so I came here."

"Is something going on in your life that might cause you to have a panic attack?" he asked.

"I'm having a panic attack?" I asked.

He nodded yes.

I'm having a panic attack, I thought as the reality of what had led up to that moment threatened to strangle me from the inside.

"So, anything you want to talk to me about?" he asked.

Where do I even begin?

Saying that the past few weeks had been difficult would have been the biggest understatement of my life. Still, they couldn't compare to what had happened that morning when I woke up to countless calls from a bunch of people telling me that my card had been declined and payment hadn't gone through. I immediately logged into my bank account and felt like someone had punched me in the stomach when I read the balance: -$1,500. *Negative balance.*

"How's that possible?" I said faintly, as if asking the computer monitor.

Things didn't add up. As I scrolled down the list of payments, I saw that rent and divorce lawyers' fees had been taken out, causing my card balance to go below zero and other purchases and scheduled payments to be declined.

I was nauseated with stress.

What do I do now?

I had never been in this situation before. While on active duty in the military, I received a paycheck on the first and the fifteenth of every month, so money had never been an issue.

I can't go ask for help.

I didn't want to tarnish the impression that other people had of me and my business because, from the outside, we were at a high. We had just won the award from Bob Evans, which had given us $25,000. We were now a nationally recognized veteran-owned brand and the praise just kept pouring in. Everyone assumed we were doing great. But what they didn't know and couldn't see was that the money we received from the grant was spent on inventory in the span of a week.

I'm an imposter, I thought as I hid my face in my hands. Then, I remembered that the week prior we had made deliveries at grocery stores, and they were supposed to pay up. Their money was going to hit my bank account soon, and all these money problems would be solved. But that hint of relief was quickly replaced by another reality check when I realized that soon wasn't going to be good enough. *I need the money right now, not soon.*

That's when the heart racing had started. It increased so quickly that I instinctively placed my right hand over my heart, as if to try and calm it down. It didn't work, so I rushed myself to the emergency room.

After the doctor took the hint that I wasn't going to open up to him about my personal troubles, he left me with, "I'll come and check on you later."

"Would you like some water, Hun?" the nurse asked as she stepped into my room.

"Yes, please," I said, clearing my voice, which sounded rather groggy.

"I thought you needed some, so I came prepared," she said, offering me a plastic cup filled halfway with water. She then glanced at the machines I was hooked up to and said, "The heart rate has slowed now, so that's good. You gave us a scare there, Hun."

"Sorry," I said in a thin voice as I sipped some water. "I think I scared myself as well."

As if able to read my mind, she grabbed my hand and said, "You know what my mee-maw used to say? There's a solution to everything. The only thing we can't solve is death." Then she winked and left the room.

There's a solution to everything. Her words—well, her mee-maw's words—echoed in my head. I stared at the ceiling of my small hospital room and thought about a solution. *How do I find a solution to what I thought was the solution?*

The main reason why I decided to leave the military as an active-duty service member was because I wanted to focus completely on Mutt's Sauce. Then I left my job at the FAA and moved back to Ohio after my assistant came to pick me up with a U-Haul truck because I wanted to focus exclusively on—you guessed it—Mutt's Sauce. I thought that diving head-first into entrepreneurship was the solution to making the business a success. I even cut back on many contracts after it was brought to my attention just how much money was going to be wasted.

The business can't sustain itself.

"Alright, since you're feeling better and your numbers have stabilized, I'm discharging you," the doctor said as he came into the room and shook me out of my rabbit hole. "Just be sure to talk to someone about what has led you to this burnout."

Burnout.

Being an entrepreneur had led me to burnout. Perhaps that meant that I wasn't good at being an entrepreneur. *Should I close the business and go back to a regular job with a steady paycheck?* I was tempted. It was the quickest solution to all my problems. Maybe my grandfather had made a mistake in choosing me to carry out his legacy. Maybe he should have left it to his son, who was a professional chef. He would have known what to do with the sauce because he knew the culinary world inside out. *I should close the business; I don't have another choice.*

As I opened the door to my new rental home in Ohio, I placed the discharge papers on the kitchen counter and just stood there. I massaged my temples and closed my eyes, trying to digest everything that had happened to me in the past few weeks: divorce, leaving my job, moving to another state, negative card balance, and an ER visit. *Yep, burnout is the most obvious place to be right now.* If what the nurse said was true and there really was a solution to everything, there had to be another way to make Mutt's Sauce work, because I couldn't fathom the idea of closing down the business. It wasn't just a condiment to me, it was my grandfather's legacy that I had been entrusted with. Closing down the business was a permanent solution to what felt like a temporary situation. I needed to turn to someone who could relate to me and cared about me. I needed to turn to my likehearted assistant.

"You OK now?" she asked after I told her what happened.

"Yeah, I'm feeling better," I said. "I just don't know what to do."

"Well, you've been mentored by some of the best people in this country," she said, as I could hear utensils clicking together, which made me assume she was preparing dinner. "What would they tell you if they knew what was going on in your life right now?"

"Keep your day job," I said so mechanically that I didn't think about the words that came out of my mouth. Then, I smiled when I remembered.

"Did you know Daymond John worked at Red Lobster when he was building FUBU?"

"Oh-kay," she said, clearly confused by how that last part related to what we were talking about. "Do you want to work at Red Lobster?"

I laughed. "Why not! I have to find a job that will help me financially sustain Mutt's Sauce as I keep building it!"

"There you go, that's a good solution," she said.

I felt instantly lighter, as I had finally crawled out from underneath the heavy rock that threatened to crush me. "I'm going to find a job!" I said out loud. "Then it'll all work out. I just need a job."

"And some food," she said. "Come on over, dinner is ready, and I've made way too much for just my husband and I."

"Be there soon," I said with a big, genuine smile on my face.

A few days later, I became a bartender and slowly but surely started making my way out of the financial trouble I had put myself in. What also helped, however, was coming to terms with a hard truth: I was not financially literate. As I started to educate myself on the financial aspects and ramifications of running a business, I discovered many things I didn't know before. For example, stores take quite some time to pay out deliveries—known as net payments—and as such, the business owner should plan accordingly when it comes to expecting income. Many important lessons were learned the hard way. But I learned them.

SECRET SAUCE: What can entrepreneurs do when experiencing burnout?

As much as I wish to write that this was the first and only time I experienced burnout during my entrepreneurial career, I can't, as it has happened many times since then. But the solution was the same every single time:

- Reach out to the like-hearted people in your life.
- Be humble and honest about what your circumstances are.
- Know when to keep going, and when you need to close down the business.

Choosing a permanent solution to a temporary situation is rarely the correct answer. Here are some more tips for dealing with entrepreneurial burnout.

Recognize the signs of burnout. Burnout often sneaks up on entrepreneurs, as the drive to succeed can sometimes eclipse the toll it takes on your mental and physical well-being. That's why it's important to learn how to recognize signs of burnout, such as chronic fatigue, lack of motivation, decreased productivity, and even feelings of hopelessness.

Embrace vulnerability. Admitting burnout can be challenging, especially when the entrepreneurial world glorifies constant hustle. But being open about your struggles is the first step toward healing. Reach out to those like-hearted individuals who understand the highs and lows of entrepreneurship.

Share the reality. When talking to your like-hearted support network, be transparent about your circumstances. Explain your challenges, whether related to the business, personal life, or both. Sharing the whole picture helps your support system offer tailored advice and insights.

Seek guidance, not just sympathy. Like-hearted people provide more than just a sympathetic ear—they offer practical guidance. Discuss strategies to manage your workload, delegate tasks, or pivot your business model. Their experience can be a valuable resource for finding solutions.

Prioritize self-care. Burnout often stems from neglecting self-care. Your like-hearted supporters will likely remind you of why you should set boundaries, take breaks, and engage in activities that recharge your energy and passion.

Reframe success and failure. Like-hearted individuals can help shift your perspective on success and failure. They remind you that setbacks are part of the journey and that prioritizing your well-being is an achievement. Their encouragement can help you break free from the perfectionism trap.

Collaborative problem-solving. Burnout can lead to feeling overwhelmed and isolated. Sharing your challenges with your like-hearted network can spark collaborative problem-solving. They may offer fresh insights, resources, or even connections that can ease the burden.

Explore adaptive strategies. Instead of immediately contemplating closing your business, explore adaptive strategies. You might consider scaling down temporarily, strategically pivoting, or seeking additional support. Like-hearted individuals can help you brainstorm and weigh these options.

Realign with purpose. Burnout often clouds your sense of purpose. Engaging with your like-hearted supporters can reignite your passion by reminding you of your initial motivations and goals. This realignment can reinvigorate your commitment to your entrepreneurial journey.

As an entrepreneur, burnout is an all-too-common challenge, but it's not insurmountable. The key to rising above it lies in your ability to lean on your like-hearted support network, to be candid about your struggles, and to embrace the healing power of connection. Remember, temporary setbacks don't define your journey; your grit, humility, and commitment to growth will genuinely shape your path.

CHAPTER FIVE

ROCK BOTTOM IS TRAUMA

"**G**o see the commander immediately," read the Sticky Note on my computer at work.

Oh gosh, what's happened now?

This had never happened before—well, not at this job anyway. I had a few years of active-duty service under my belt at that point, and I had mainly served as an acquisitions officer, known in the civilian world as a program manager. As an Air Force officer, I worked in the corporate world, and other servicemembers often teased those of us who did by calling us "chairborne rangers" as opposed to "airborne rangers," because we spent our time sitting behind desks in an office environment as opposed to going down range in combat zones. The term never really bothered me because I knew that each one of us in the force played a pivotal role in carrying out the mission. However, I never really grasped the magnitude of what that meant until 2008, when I read that Sticky Note.

At the time, I was the program manager for what is now known as the Modular Aerial Fire Fighting System (MAFFS), the "leading provider of modular aerial firefighting systems and technologies in the world." The program started in "1971 as a joint effort between the U.S. Forest Service and the

Department of Defense to produce the equipment, training and operational procedures to integrate military air tankers into a national firefighting response." Over the past fifty years, MAFFS has "become the leading provider of modular aerial firefighting systems for militaries and communities around the globe."[5] Basically, my job consisted of overseeing and coordinating everything associated with this firefighting system that involved a tank of fire retardant. The tank would be loaded into the back of a military C-130 transport plane and deployed when a state requested federal aid to fight wildland forest fires.

"We've received an email from Governor Schwarzenegger in California, and he's called for federal support," the commander said after I entered his office and saluted him. "He's saying that California is burning down right now, people are losing their homes and their lives are at risk because of this fire that they can't contain. You're the only one with a firefighting program on active duty so we need your help."

I blinked twice. *Did I hear him right?* I was in my twenties and my job, up until then, had indeed consisted of being in an office environment. Now, all of a sudden I would be directly responsible for *saving lives.*

"Wh-what am I supposed to do?" I asked the commander, trying my best to appear calm, cool, and collected.

"The mission is clear," he said without flinching. "Put out this fire. So, go ahead and coordinate with teams of reserves, active duty, the US Forest Service, and our lead command, Air Force Materiel Command, and do so as fast as possible. Also, you're going to have to help update the media on procedures and how the operations are coming along, so you'll have to prepare statements for leadership to release to the press."

---

5. Description taken from MAFFS website homepage, accessed July 21, 2023, https://www.maffs.com/.

For the next few days, I worked on this mission nonstop. My days consisted of coordinating the mission and my nights were all about writing statements that would be sent to the press the next day. I slept and ate very little, but it didn't matter because the mission came first. People's lives were at risk, and we needed all hands on deck. The news about the California wildfires took the nation by storm and the media coverage was constant. "With eight MAFFS-capable C-130s in the 302nd AEG, Airmen will launch as many missions as California officials require to contain the wildfires," the Air Force website stated in an article as we entered the fifth day of operations. "Aircrews have dropped approximately 117,000 gallons of fire retardant since airborne missions began June 26. The C-130s are based in Sacramento and allow the aircraft to fly with maximum fuel loads and operate MAFFS with full fire retardant capability."[6]

Eventually, the fires were extinguished, and I could breathe a sigh of relief. However, in the aftermath of that mission, I realized that I had been responsible for someone else's life. Do you know how that feels? If I didn't move fast enough, someone could have died. It weighed heavily on me, but I didn't have that much time to dwell on it or process those emotions because, in the military, once you do a good job, they keep tasking you with more and more responsibilities because you've proved yourself to be trustworthy. This is a good thing, of course, something that makes me proud. But each new job assigned to me carried even more crucial responsibilities, way heavier than those experienced in the past. Due to multiple reasons, I cannot reveal what those jobs

---

6. Senior Airman Stephen Collier, "Airmen launch fifth day of California fire support," 302nd Air Expeditionary Group Public Affairs, July 1, 2008, accessed July 21, 2023, https://www.af.mil/News/Article-Display/Article/123116/airmen-launch-fifth-day-of-california-fire-support/.

or responsibilities were—ever, to anyone. But I will say that I have been deployed and there are so many things going on in the world that civilians are not aware of and will never see happening. Given the magnitude of those experiences, keeping the details bottled up inside without having the freedom of sharing them with other people (not even with a therapist), can lead to serious consequences. One of them, for me, was a mystery illness while I was deployed. Out of nowhere, I fell ill with symptoms that resembled food poisoning. I couldn't hold down water. Days turned into weeks, and then months. However, doctors were baffled and didn't know what they were dealing with: Was it stomach flu? Was it anxiety? Was it undiagnosed post-traumatic stress disorder (PTSD)? Was I poisoned? They never figured it out.

"Listen, this could be related to the anxiety problems you have," one doctor said, almost in hushed tones as if he didn't want anyone to hear. "You should really go to a therapist so they can diagnose you with whatever it is that is afflicting you so badly."

Yeah, and if they diagnose me with PTSD, who is ever going to promote an officer with that acronym on her record?

Meanwhile, I still had to report to my follow-on assignment, and not just any job. I have it written in black and white on my performance report, where I had been rated number one, that I had tackled the hardest job of an O-3 (captain) in the whole command. The same year I spent at that job I went to the ER twenty-three times. Ultimately, they decided all they could do was medicate to maintain, so they put me on nausea medicine that they give to cancer patients going through chemotherapy. This happened in 2010. I have been on that medication ever since.

I never sought help until well after leaving the service. I reached out to the Veterans Affairs and filed for disability (I now have a disability rating of 70 percent). With their help, I began unpacking a lot of things that I didn't know had been there this entire time. I thought that my trauma had started while serving in the military and experiencing hardships I could never share with anyone. Instead, I found out that my upbringing had been a constant battle against the odds: raised by a single mother, moved to the projects, and part of a minority. The odds were so many that, statistically speaking, I should never have been successful. Fighting against those statistics, never feeling like I could finally take a breather, compounded the issue. So, when I began my military service, I had already been living with anxiety—unbeknownst to me. But once I reached out for help and began unpacking every single layer that made me who I am (even though there were still things I couldn't talk about), it helped me face my traumas and give them proper names. This knowledge and awareness allowed me to regain control over my emotions and my circumstances. I then had the tools to prepare a game plan.

SECRET SAUCE: How can entrepreneurs tackle trauma so that it doesn't prevent them from moving forward with their entrepreneurial goals?

First of all, it's important that you become aware of your own trauma. Trauma has many faces: It can be caused by something that happened during childhood, by an adult relationship gone bad, or even by a natural disaster. Whatever trauma you are facing, you must put in the work to recognize it and learn how to keep living alongside it. My past traumas will never go away, and probably neither will yours. They will always be part of us. But the difference between who I was and who I am now is that I no longer run away from or ignore them. Rather, I acknowledge them and am able to keep moving forward while carrying them along for the ride. And that's the real superpower.

Traumatic experiences can cast long shadows in the complex entrepreneurship landscape, impacting personal well-being and business pursuits. Addressing trauma head-on is crucial for entrepreneurs to maintain balance and regain momentum. Discover practical strategies to confront and transcend trauma, allowing personal growth to flourish alongside entrepreneurial ambitions.

Confront the reality. Begin your growth process by acknowledging the presence of trauma. Identify the specific experiences that have left a lasting impact. This step is fundamental to moving forward with a clear understanding of your challenges. Military veterans are especially prone to one behavior: compartmentalization. We put all our trauma and emotions "in a box" in order to get the mission done. The problem is, at some point, the box becomes too full to hold it all, leading to breakdowns of every kind.

Seek professional support. Trauma can be intricate and deeply rooted. Engage with therapists or counselors experienced in trauma recovery. Their insights provide tailored strategies to navigate personal and business healing complexities. Therapy isn't a fad. It's healthy to reach out for help.

Embrace mindfulness and self-care. Integrate mindfulness practices into your routine. Techniques like meditation, deep breathing, and self-reflection foster self-awareness and help manage overwhelming emotions associated with trauma.

Establish boundaries. Setting clear boundaries in personal and business contexts safeguards your well-being. By clearly defining limits, you create space for healing without succumbing to additional stressors. People who really care about you will respect those boundaries. When you start changing habits and leveling up, it will expose all the people who benefitted from your lack of boundaries. Your circle may get smaller, but the quality will increase.

Leverage social support. Connect with friends, family members, mentors, or fellow entrepreneurs who provide understanding and empathy. Sharing your experience with those who empathize can provide relief and perspective.

Encourage open communication. Create an environment encouraging open conversations about trauma. Transparency within your support network—personal and professional—aids mutual understanding and fosters a sense of community.

Engage in therapeutic activities. Channel your energy into creative outlets that resonate with you. Engaging in activities like writing, art, music, or even physical exercise can be cathartic, helping you to process and release trauma-associated emotions.

Utilize strategic planning. Apply your problem-solving skills to your healing journey. Develop a strategic plan that outlines steps to address trauma and track progress. Treating it like a business challenge can empower you to take control.

Explore new perspectives. Seek inspiration from your journey. Consider how your experience can reshape your approach to entrepreneurship. Your unique insights may drive innovation and lead to more empathetic business solutions.

Cultivate patience. Healing takes time—in your business and personal life. Acknowledge that progress might be gradual. Practicing patience empowers you to approach healing with a long-term perspective.

Learn from the experience. Extract valuable lessons from your traumatic experience. Reflect on how it has shaped your resilience, empathy, and problem-solving skills. Apply these newfound qualities to your entrepreneurial endeavors.

Pivot with purpose. Trauma can be a catalyst for change. Consider adapting your business model to align with your transformed perspective. Using adversity as a springboard, you can develop ventures that make a positive impact.

Navigating trauma requires a multi-faceted approach, blending professional guidance, self-care practices, and open communication. By embracing these strategies, you pave the way for healing while keeping your entrepreneurial aspirations alive. Remember, healing from trauma doesn't detract from your business journey; it enhances it, allowing you to harness your experiences as a source of strength and insight.

PART II:
ROCK BOTTOM IS SOCIAL

CHAPTER SIX

ROCK BOTTOM IS DIVERSITY

The first rays of the morning sun shyly peeked through the white clouds. I closed my eyes and tilted my face toward them to greet them. *I am exactly where I'm supposed to be.* I smiled. I lowered my chin and looked at my camouflage blouse. *I am a United States Air Force cadet!*

It was my first week of boot camp and they had been working us hard—there is a reason why it's called Hell Week. But I had been keeping up with everything they had us do and I had even been named cadet commander of all the cadets at Lackland Air Force Base. Since it was only our first week of boot camp though, none of us knew what to do, so we all got into our fair share of troubles when we accidentally did something wrong. But that was to be expected, and I took mine with dignity and no complaints. After all, my grandfather had told me so many wonderful things about the military and how he believed that the Air Force was the best branch of all. He described it as the perfect world, where people looked after one another, where the uniform made you all belong together, and where you were bonded by a shared mission—an important mission. And if my grandfather believed that the Air Force was the most evolved of the branches, I had no reason not to trust him. He had fought in the Vietnam War and come back to a country that did not even recognize him as a full citizen—the same country he had vowed to defend and could have potentially died for while out in the field. He walked around with one kneecap and a ton of undiagnosed PTSD due to his service in the Vietnam era. So if he said that the Air Force was this idyllic place, it must have been, because he saw the worst of the worst.

And he didn't just talk about it; he had photos to prove his theory. There was one photo in particular of him surrounded by many other enlisted people, all from different cultural backgrounds. The photo captures a moment in time when they were all hanging out as friends at a cookout in Okinawa, Japan, and everyone is smiling and having a good time. He took great pride in the fact that his sauce could bring people together, and by doing so, break down racial barriers that were still so predominant in both the military and the civilian world. His own call sign, "Mutt," made it clear that he was able to blend in with just about everyone. And I was finally part of that world too!

I had been living and breathing this utopia for a week when an officer asked me, "What's that purple shit in your hair?"

Wait, what?

I had no idea what he was talking about, but he was staring at my hair. My brain quickly ran a scan of all the possible issues he could have been referring to: *Is my hair purple?* Of course not. My hair is brown.

Is my hair out of regulation? Absolutely not. Sure, I was a brand-new cadet, but I would never make such a rookie mistake. There are very strict rules one must follow when it comes to personal grooming in the military. As a Black woman, I was allowed to keep my hair in braids, which was the style I had chosen to keep it in—in the Texas heat and humidity there was no way my hair was going to remain manageable otherwise, and the G.I. Jane look, I felt, didn't really suit me.

So, if my hair met regulations, what was he referring to?

I didn't have to wait long for him to make it clear.

"This isn't the ghetto," he said right in my face. "If you're going to be an officer, you have to act like you didn't come from it."

Air.

I felt like I had just got punched in the stomach and I couldn't breathe.

No, no, don't let them out. I said to myself as tears began rushing to my eyes.

I wanted to fold over in pain because I felt as if something inside of me had imploded. Something that could never be repaired because it had been shattered into a million different pieces. That something was the promise of a world that my grandfather believed existed. A world that saw no color, just human beings united by a vow of protecting the greatest country in the world. I couldn't process the magnitude of that destroyed promise.

That same evening, I had some of my fellow female cadets help me cut all my braids. With every braid cut, a little piece of my innocence (or maybe I should call it "naivety") went with it. I had received a major rude awakening and my eyes were now open to the reality that racism existed also in the most perfect of military branches. Not only did I feel mortified by the experience I had been subjected to, but also exhausted.

I had fought against racism my entire life. As a Black girl growing up in the South, I lived racism every single day. I won't go into all the details (as they would turn into a whole different book), but just to give you an idea of what my life was like, many of my former high school soccer friends have a shared memory of the team from Pulaski, Tennessee calling me the N-word throughout the game instead of my uniform number. I was the only Black girl on the field. What hurt me so much was not just the way they referred to me—which was the most dehumanizing experience—but the fact that so many adults stood around and heard people calling me that and the game didn't stop. I had never felt so—*other*. My teammates were horrified and the bus ride was very solemn, but there was no real reprimand for the opposing team. Let that sink in.

At the beginning of the first week of boot camp, I thought racism had no place on the other side of the gate that protects the military base—certainly not in 2002. Clearly, I couldn't have been more wrong. I wish I could say that this was the first and only time somebody in the military made me feel wrong for the way my hair looked, but that would be a lie. You see, the pressure to assimilate and hide my natural hair (as if it were something to be ashamed of) came from the worst person it could have ever come from: a Black man. I had been dating this military service member, and one day, I told him, "I am so done doing this to my hair."

"What do you mean?" he said.

"I straighten my hair with all these chemicals and they're doing nothing but damage to it," I said. "Not to mention the health risks these chemicals could bring to me in the long run."

"But if you don't straighten it, what are you going to do to it?" he asked, a hint of confusion in his voice.

I shrugged and said, "I'm going to go natural. I am going to cut it off, so it grows back healthier." It was the most obvious choice.

He didn't reply right away. Instead, he looked like he had just smelled something bad, the way he wrinkled his nose.

"What is it?" I asked. *Now I'm confused.*

"I don't know if that's the right thing to do," he said, looking away from me.

"You mean for the military? Nah, I checked regulations, I'll be fine if I style it in a certain way." I was about to walk away and head to the kitchen because to me, this conversation was over. Certainly, that was the only thing he must have been concerned about.

Right?

Wrong!

"I don't mean the regulations," he said. "I mean, me."

I stopped walking and turned slowly to face him, but his eyes wouldn't meet mine.

"Explain," I said.

"I am not attracted to natural hair. And when I met you, your hair was straight. I like it the way it is."

Boom!

Another implosion.

"W-what do you mean?" I asked. My mouth was so dry that pronouncing those words felt like chewing on sandpaper.

"Just what I said."

Maybe he misunderstood.

I took my phone and scrolled through some old photos of mine until I found the one I had been looking for. *Surely this is going to change his mind.*

"Look," I said, walking closer to him and showing him the photo of me sporting my natural hair. "This is how it's going to look."

He's going to be relieved now and apologize.

The corners of my lips curled upward as I saw his eyes leave the phone screen and slowly meet mine. *Here comes the apology.*

"What did I do to you to deserve this?" He furrowed his brows.

He was not apologetic. He was not remorseful. He was dead serious.

He took the photo as a way for me to punish him.

A Black man, a military man I was dating, did not want to see me with my natural hair. I had never felt so unattractive before. This man was supposed to know that this is how I, *we*, are made. We are born with this hair texture, and for him to say that he is not attracted to the natural version of me was more hurtful than when that officer told me I looked like I came from the ghetto.

The next day, I put on my uniform and went to work. And did so for many years, trying to survive an environment that wanted the best version of me while beating me down for being born this way.

Eventually, I reached a point in my entrepreneurial career when I thought to myself, *Enough, Charlynda!* It was time for me to accept my hair. It was time for me to believe that I didn't need to assimilate to be valuable. It was time for me to embrace who I truly was regardless of what other people thought. I won't lie, it took me many years, and it's still a work in progress. But I know I am growing as an individual and entrepreneur because owning who I am, has turned that rock bottom into the best trampoline!

SECRET SAUCE: How can entrepreneurs turn their own insecurities into their strength?

Insecurity comes in many shapes and forms. As you've learned, I was insecure about my hair, so I modified it any way I could to assimilate and not stand out. While hair is something that is visible, many other types of insecurities are not. You can't tell just by looking at somebody if they suffer from PTSD or if they have ADHD, for example. Until they decide to confess it and own up to it. As an entrepreneur, being transparent about who you are and what you stand for can truly be a superpower. People are so tired of perfection and don't connect with it because they can't relate. *Fake it 'till you make it* is no longer cool. Keep it real. They want to connect with people who are flawed, who have failed, who have faltered. Basically, they want to connect with other human beings. If you are strong enough to show them your vulnerability, then you will connect with your target audience in a way that perhaps you have never experienced before. Though the path to self-acceptance and self-love can often last a lifetime, I believe it is the most valuable journey we could possibly embark upon. Not just as entrepreneurs, but as human beings.

Diversity, both visible and invisible, is a cornerstone of the human experience, and for entrepreneurs, embracing this diversity within themselves can be a powerful catalyst for personal growth and business success. Turning insecurities into strengths involves a journey of self-acceptance and transparency that resonates deeply with others. As you've discovered, this journey goes beyond physical appearances; it extends to mental and emotional well-being complexities. Here are some thoughts to help you embrace yourself and your diversity.

Embrace your unique identity. Be proud of what makes you stand out, whether that is your cultural heritage, your neurodiversity, your unique abilities, or your sexual orientation. Be proud of who you are and where you come from. Heavy is the invisible weight of being "the only one" or the "token." To make an impact, however, someone has to be first. Someone has to be in the room. You may feel like you're living life in a box right now. I'm here to tell you it may be time to bust it wide open and forget the standards.

Diversity encompasses every aspect of you, from your background and experiences to your strengths and vulnerabilities. Embrace your uniqueness and recognize that your insecurities contribute to the rich tapestry that makes you who you are.

Acknowledge and understand your insecurities. Self-awareness is key. Reflect on the origins of your insecurities and how they've shaped your perception of yourself. Understand that everyone has insecurities; they are a natural part of the human experience.

Foster self-compassion. Treat yourself with the kindness you would offer a friend. Instead of allowing insecurities to breed self-criticism, use them as an opportunity to practice self-compassion and cultivate a more nurturing relationship with yourself.

Leverage vulnerability for connection. Authenticity is a magnet for connection in entrepreneurship. Share your vulnerabilities, whether visible or hidden, with your audience. This transparency fosters a genuine connection that resonates deeply with others.

Challenge perceptions of perfection. Society often idealizes perfection, but real connection flourishes in imperfection. Break down the barrier of a polished facade and allow others to see the genuine human behind the entrepreneur. Authenticity cultivates trust.

Inspire others through your journey. Your willingness to navigate your insecurities and share your progress inspires others to embark on their journeys of self-acceptance. As an entrepreneur, you have a platform to be a role model for positive change.

Build an inclusive business culture. Entrepreneurship allows you to shape the culture of your business. Create an environment where employees, partners, and customers feel valued for who they are. Remember, people don't leave bad companies, they leave bad leaders (bosses).

Leverage empathy in your business strategy. Understanding the struggles of others can give you a unique edge in business. Your journey of embracing diversity and confronting insecurities equips you with empathy, helping you design products and services that genuinely address people's needs.

Connect with your target audience. Transparency about your challenges resonates deeply with those who face similar struggles. By sharing your vulnerabilities, you create an avenue for meaningful conversations and connections.

Prioritize self-care. Embracing diversity within yourself includes prioritizing your mental, emotional, and physical well-being. Taking care of yourself enhances your ability to navigate insecurities and become a strong, authentic entrepreneur.

Celebrate growth and learning. View your journey as a continuous process of growth and learning. Every step toward self-acceptance and vulnerability contributes to personal development and enhances entrepreneurial impact.

Insecurities need not hold entrepreneurs back; they can be catalysts for personal empowerment and professional success. As you embrace your diversity, visible and invisible, you empower others to do the same. Through your authenticity, you build a strong foundation for your entrepreneurial endeavors and contribute to a more inclusive and empathetic business landscape. Remember, your journey of self-acceptance isn't just a path to entrepreneurship; it's a universal journey that has the potential to inspire and uplift countless individuals on their paths of growth.

CHAPTER SEVEN

ROCK BOTTOM IS SOCIAL MEDIA

I'm *going to delete all of my social media*, I thought as the backlash kept coming. *What have I gotten myself into?*

I got up from my computer and left my phone on the desk, by the keyboard. I had to put some physical distance between social media and myself in the hope that it would help clear my mind—and slow down my heartbeat, which had been increasing as quickly as the online haters.

All I wanted to do was help her . . . but it had backfired big time.

It all started when, just a few days prior, I had come across a video of a woman who wanted to sell her homemade sauce online. She was receiving so much praise because the sauce and concept was captivating, but as a fellow entrepreneur, I noticed quite a few things in her videos that she didn't seem to be paying attention to. So, I did what my mama taught me to do: extend a helping hand. After all, she was in the food (sauce, to be precise) business, and so was I. It made sense for me to reach out, right?

I left a few comments with suggestions on how to improve her business model and ways to increase production and sales. At first, the feedback on those comments was positive, as people were praising me for supporting another self-made woman. Those pats on the shoulder made me feel good because I felt valuable: I was using the many rock bottoms I had encountered throughout my entrepreneurial journey to help another female entrepreneur—and hopefully prevent her from making the same mistakes.

So, you see, everything was going well. Until it wasn't.

It didn't take long for the negative comments to pop up. I was pelted with accusations of wanting to sabotage her business, accusations of not knowing what I was talking about, and accusations of buying into and supporting her narrative—thus making me just as wrong as she was about what she was doing with her business. The hate was real. At first, I tried to defend myself by replying to these comments, even making videos in which I explained myself, so people knew why I had written what I had written. But the more I explained myself, the more hate I received. Soon, people started attacking Mutt's Sauce by default, because as its owner, me and my company were one and the same.

That's when I thought that the best solution was for me to delete all my social media platforms. Now that Mutt's Sauce had been dragged into this nasty online bashing, I couldn't risk getting any dirt on the company that I had built from scratch with blood, sweat, and tears. I had worked too hard to let it sink like that. Not to mention how much I valued my grandfather's legacy, which was now at stake.

Staring into nothing, I walked back and forth, back and forth, trying to find a way to get out of this mess. Deleting social media seemed the quickest and easiest solution, but I knew that, no matter what, once something is online, it is always going to stay online. The internet is forever. My online platform has always been extremely valuable to me because it's how I connect with my customers. Also, in my experience, the quickest and easiest solution is hardly the best one to go with.

So what should I do? This was uncharted territory for me as I had never found myself in the crossfire before.

"What are you doing?" my mother said, startling me.

I turned to look at her and she was standing by the threshold, holding grocery bags.

"Oh, hey, how long have you been standing there for?" I asked.

"Enough to see you walk around lookin' crazy," she said, stepping inside the house and closing the door behind her.

I went to help her with the bags and placed them on the kitchen counter.

"Thank you for buying all these groceries for me," I said.

"You're welcome," she said, placing the dozen eggs in the fridge. "Now can you tell me why you were walking like a caged animal?"

I sighed heavily and told her what had happened.

"So, what are you going to do about it?" she asked, all the groceries now placed where they were supposed to be.

"That's the thing, I have no idea." I sat down on the couch, elbows on my legs, holding my chin with both hands. "I've never been in this situation before."

"I know you haven't," she said, sitting next to me on the couch and moving my hands so I'd have to hold my own head up. "But you're certainly not the first entrepreneur to find themselves in this situation."

"What do you mean?" I said, looking at her.

"Think about it: How many entrepreneurs have found themselves in the crossfire? Do some research, see what they did or said and how they solved the situation—if they did."

I quickly got up and walked to the desk to get my phone.

What other entrepreneurs have found themselves in this sort of situation? I didn't have to dig that deep.

"Quite a few, actually," I said, still scrolling through my phone but talking to my mom. "Many of them succumbed to the crossfire while others survived it."

"And what is that those who succeeded did but those who succumbed did not?" she asked.

"I don't know," I said, focusing on a few stories.

"Take your time to figure it out," she said. "I'm sure this is not about reinventing the wheel. If there's one thing I've learned it's that no matter what you go through, there is always somebody who's been there before and has written about it to show you how to get through it as well."

"Wait," I said, focusing on a story in particular. "I think the key is to just own up to what you did or said and move on."

"Acknowledge your mistake and move on, huh?" she said. "Sounds like a good solution to me."

"But do you really think that all of these people who've been bashing me online are going to disappear once I do that?" I looked at her, wanting to see a yes in her eyes. Instead—

"Of course not, there is always going to be that 80 percent of people who just can't do anything but talk trash about you," she said, standing up and walking up to me.

"So, what do I do?" I asked, feeling like the hint of hope I felt only moments ago had already left my body.

"Hold on to the remaining 20 percent," she said, offering a sweet and reassuring smile. "No matter what you do, there are always going to be people who complain about you. But there's also always going to be people there to support you and love what you do."

She's right.

"I guess I'm about to go live on social media and make my peace with this story then," I said, smiling back at her.

"That's my girl," she said. Then, before I began the livestream, she wished me a good day and went about her life.

I took a deep breath and went live.

What happened after the video was what I expected to happen: Some people supported me while others did not. But I did what my mother told me and decided to hang on to the 20 percent. After all, it is with like-hearted people that I grow the most.

SECRET SAUCE: How can entrepreneurs survive a social media backlash?

Social media is a double-edged sword. Most businesses need it to engage their target market and keep steady communication with customers. It's proven, time and time again, to be one of the most efficient, quickest ways to grow a business. For these and many other reasons, social media has become invaluable to most entrepreneurs. However, it has also been the stage to many businesspeople's swan song. All it takes is one like, one comment, one share, or one post of the wrong content and *boom!* People are going to immediately come after you, holding you accountable and questioning your integrity. When you become an entrepreneur, it becomes close to impossible to keep separation between you the human being and you the brand. The best way to turn this—very public—rock bottom into a trampoline is to own your mistakes, learn from them, and move on.

Surviving a social media backlash is a skill every entrepreneur should master in the digital age. While the benefits of social media for business are undeniable, its pitfalls can be equally impactful. As an entrepreneur, it's crucial to understand how to weather the storm of negative attention and transform adversity into an opportunity for growth. These principles will help you get started.

Embrace proactive crisis management. Prepare for potential backlash by developing a crisis management strategy in advance. Identify potential trigger points, have contingency plans, and ensure you can respond swiftly and decisively if a crisis arises.

Cultivate a calm disposition. Negative comments and backlash can be emotionally taxing, but composure is paramount. Your emotions are seen before they are heard. We've all seen posts shared by people while they're still emotionally charged—the term "unhinged" is usually an apt description of these. Cultivate the ability to handle criticism without being reactive or defensive.

Monitor and be present. Regularly monitor your social media channels or hire a social media manager to catch negative feedback early. Engaging with your positive and negative audience shows your commitment to addressing concerns.

Respond authentically and transparently. If you make a mistake, acknowledge it openly and in a timely manner. Craft sincere, transparent responses that show you're taking responsibility. Being genuine in your apology can defuse tensions and earn respect.

Take conversations offline. Consider moving conversations to private messages or emails if negative feedback escalates. Doing so allows you to address concerns more personally and prevents public spats from spiraling out of control. On a legal note, documentation can save you if it wades into dangerous waters, like defamation of character or accusations of fraud. Make a habit of keeping a paper trail. You don't need to show your receipts to your social media followers to prove your point. Just hang on to them in case a lawyer is involved.

Learn and adapt. Every setback is an opportunity for growth. Analyze the situation objectively, identify areas of improvement, and apply these lessons moving forward.

Encourage constructive dialogue. Turn negative feedback into a chance for meaningful conversations. Ask probing questions and listen to understand the concerns of your audience. Your followers will see your commitment to improvement.

Seek allies amongst the criticism. Not all feedback is negative; some individuals may offer valuable insights for improvement. Identify those genuinely interested in helping you grow and engage with them constructively.

Showcase examples of positive impact. Share stories of how your business positively impacts customers, employees, or the community. Demonstrating your commitment to making a difference can counterbalance negative perceptions.

Evolve and adapt. Social media backlash can be a catalyst for change. Use it to reassess your brand's messaging, values, and strategies and make necessary adjustments.

Build a loyal support network. Surround yourself with a network of mentors, fellow entrepreneurs, or friends who will provide you with a different perspective and not just pacify you. Let them play devil's advocate and give you the worst-case scenario.

Reframe the narrative. Social media backlash can redefine your brand narrative. Turn negative incidents into stories of resilience, growth, and redemption that inspire others.

Embracing challenges, including social media backlash, is integral to an entrepreneur's journey. Rather than allowing negative experiences to define you, view them as stepping stones to further success. By demonstrating authenticity, accountability, and a commitment to learning from mistakes, you not only navigate social media storms but also emerge stronger, wiser, and more attuned to your audience's needs. Remember, turning adversity into triumph is a testament to your ability to thrive in the dynamic world of entrepreneurship.

CHAPTER EIGHT

ROCK BOTTOM IS PEER PRESSURE

"**H**i Charlynda, this is Daymond John."

OK, I know this chapter has just started, but let's pause here for a minute, shall we? I want you to picture the scene: It was four years after I had gone on *Shark Tank*, where I wanted to pitch to Daymond John (but he wasn't there, remember?), and I was walking in the FAA building where I worked, minding my own business. Suddenly, my phone rang. It was an unknown number from New York. *Who's calling me from New York?* I thought. My first instinct was to let the call go to voicemail. But then I remembered something important. *It could be someone from Bob Evans calling me to talk logistics for the event in New York.* So, I answered with the all-too-common, rather unassuming, "Hello?"

And that's when I heard his voice say the sentence that I opened this chapter with.

I pride myself on being a humble-but-strong woman who has faced whatever life has thrown at her with her head held up high. Nothing in life was ever handed to me—aside from the envelope containing my grandfather's sauce recipe, that is. I had to fight tooth and nail to get to where I am in life. So, you can imagine just how surprised—actually, shocked—I was when my reaction to hearing that sentence was not one of composure; it was not one of professionalism; it was not one of entrepreneurial integrity. Nope, none of that. My reaction was completely out of left field.

I sobbed!

I completely fell apart while on the phone with him. I started crying, my mascara started running, and Daymond John started saying, "Take a deep breath." It took me a while and a whole lot of introspection to figure out why my reaction was uncontrollable crying, but when I finally was able to sit down with that emotion and call the culprit by its own name, I learned that it was *peer pressure*.

To properly explain how I got to the moment when my emotions succumbed to peer pressure, I need to take you several steps back.

"There is this new conference happening here in Dallas, Texas, we should go," my friend Molly Mae told me in 2017.

"What type of conference is it?" I asked her over the phone.

"It's for influencers," she said. "It's called 'Military Influencer Conference,' and I'm telling you, it's going to be big!"

Molly and I had become very good friends since competing in the 2016 Ms. Veteran America contest, in which she won the title and I was the runner-up. With names like Molly Mae and Charlynda Jean, it felt destined that we would end up as best friends.

"Alright, let's do it," I said.

Soon, we were sitting in the conference room in Dallas, listening to inspirational speakers tell their stories of how they went from being veterans to entrepreneurs—and not just any entrepreneurs, these were people whose companies had hit the million-dollar mark. It was a wonderful event with many networking experiences that somehow put even more pressure on me. You see, I started my company around the same time that some of the entrepreneurs who spoke at this conference did. But Mutt's Sauce had yet to reach the million-dollar mark. *Peer pressure.*

Also, while competing, building a brand and a legacy, and settling into my new role of military spouse and former active-duty Air Force officer, I had also been trying to become a mother. Most of my peers had settled down and started families. Some of them had not even been married for as long as I had been and were already parents to at least two children. The longer I went without having a baby, the more people would ask me, "So, when are you going to have a baby?" And every time, that question felt like a dagger to my chest. Though my then-husband and I had tried for years, I couldn't get pregnant. My body just wouldn't cooperate. I went to countless doctors, and nothing helped. So, while on the outside I looked like I had it all together—a successful marriage, a high-powered career, and enough time on my hands to compete and go to conferences—internally I felt like a complete and utter failure. Insert irrational thought: *I had failed as a wife and as a woman because I couldn't get pregnant.* Why were so many other women I knew already mothers but not me? *Peer pressure.*

Anyway, after the conference ended, we attendees kept in touch through a private Facebook group where we exchanged ideas, supported one another, and shared leads. Basically, it was peer networking on steroids.

"Hey, don't know if anybody has heard about Bob Evans Heroes to CEOs, but it's important that as many people as possible in this group apply for this grant," wrote a member. "Oh, I think the deadline is today."

As soon as I read the message on the group, I quickly went to the grant website and applied. Fortunately, I had all the necessary material ready, including a video in which I shared the story of Mutt's Sauce, so it didn't take me long to complete the application. Once I hit *Send,* I went on about my life and for weeks didn't hear anything about the application status.

That is, until I was notified that I had won the grand prize, which consisted of a $25,000 grant, plus one-on-one mentorship with none other than Daymond John. I could not believe it! Four years later, when I received that call from Daymond John, I felt like my life had come full circle. After I finally calmed down and pulled myself together, he told me that he was looking forward to meeting me in New York for the ceremony.

Fast-forward to the day I finally met him in person. After touring the USS *Intrepid*, the ceremony began with each mentor introducing their mentees.

"Charlynda, I think you broke into tears when I called you," Daymond John said as he began his introduction.

Cue the laughter from the audience.

"Yeah . . . " I said, my voice low in an attempt not to let others hear me. But, of course, they did. Cue even more laughter.

"When Charlynda Scales followed in her grandfather's footsteps and chose to serve in the Air Force, little did she know that she was following his footsteps in another important endeavor: starting a business," he said to the now engaged, but quiet, audience. "In 1956, Charlynda's grandfather, Charlie "Mutt" Ferrell, Jr., decided that he had had enough of using all sorts of condiments for each dish that he created his own sauce that could go with every single meal. So, Mutt's Sauce, named after Charlie, is a multi-purpose condiment which infuses sweet, tangy, and a little heat into each spoonful. Charlynda was close to her grandfather and when he passed away, he left her the heavily guarded secret recipe. Charlynda founded Mutt's Sauce to bring the delicious sauce to the world. Soon, you will see Mutt's Sauce on tables all over America. Charlynda, congratulations. Come on up."

I got up and walked to the stage where Daymond John stood. Accompanied by a loud applause, I felt like I was floating on clouds as I moved.

This is it. I am finally going to reach the goals I have been working so hard for since I was entrusted with the recipe. In that moment, I felt like I had it all. A wonderful family who had supported me through thick and thin, a loving husband who proudly smiled while watching me walk up to Daymond John, and a successful business that was about to take the country by storm.

Once I got on stage, I thanked Daymond John for the speech and the support, and I was officially given the check for $25,000. Then, it was time for the one-on-one mentorship session.

"Charlynda, he's waiting for you in there," one of the organizers told me, nodding toward a room.

"Thank you," I said and made my way there.

I opened the door and was stunned by what I saw. Or better, by what I didn't see. I knew this was a one-on-one session, but I never expected it to be so . . . empty. I blinked twice to make sure that my eyes were not deceiving me. They weren't. In that room were two chairs—one of them occupied by my mentor. A cameraman was there, and Daymond's manager was quietly typing emails on his cell phone in the corner. That was it. I don't know what I was expecting, perhaps more people present, or more furniture. But I just didn't picture the ambience to be so minimalistic.

"Come on in," he said, shaking me out of my momentary interior design analysis. "Take a seat."

I accepted his invitation and sat down.

"What questions do you have for me?" he asked.

Straight to the point. Once again, I was caught off guard. I don't know what I was expecting—certainly I didn't think we would start the session by talking about the weather—but everything around me, including his demeanor, which was welcoming and professional, made me understand this was the time to show up and show out. *Let's do this!*

"As you know, Mutt's Sauce started with my grandfather," I said, looking straight at him. "Family is the most important thing to me. I am not just building Mutt's Sauce for my own sake. I want this to be a company that can last the test of time." He nodded, which told me he understood where I was going with this. "Do you plan on turning FUBU into a company that provides multigenerational wealth? Will you leave FUBU to your kids?" I was of course referring to the apparel company he and three other friends founded and launched in 1992: For Us, By Us (FUBU).

He smiled and began advising me on steps to take to properly scale a food company and what involvement family should reasonably have in the process.

"Next?" he asked, referring to the next question.

"Well, my goal is to be in brick-and-mortar stores," I said, adjusting myself on the chair to get a bit more comfortable since I was feeling more relaxed. "Do you have any recommendations for me on how to go about it and avoid common pitfalls?"

"The most important thing is to have inventory, but not too much inventory." He said, "And the manufacturing capability to sustain the demand."

Our conversation lasted about an hour, and it was packed with information that I believe would have taken me years to gather on my own—and probably a whole lot of setbacks. It was also during that conversation that I learned he had been working on a new book—he's a prolific author, so the news of an upcoming new release didn't surprise me.

"What's the title of the book?" I asked him.

"*Rise and Grind*," he said.

"Seriously?" I couldn't believe it. "I use that expression all the time!"

"See, great minds think alike," he said. "I'm actually looking for ambassadors for my book, including VIP ambassadors, but that window is almost closed."

VIP ambassador. If I were to become one, that would allow me to keep in touch with him way beyond this Bob Evans grant. I have got to become one!

Of course, the Inner Critic crept up on me and told me that I was never going to be accepted because I was sure to be up against some serious, serious competition. But this time, I didn't listen to that voice. I decided to shoot my shot. After my mentoring, I walked over to his manager.

"Well, now that you have three winners of the national contest for veteran entrepreneurs, I think it would be great if I could be one of the VIP ambassadors," I said.

What was the worst that could happen? He could have said, "Thank you, but no."

What was the best that could happen? He could have accepted my pitch and granted me VIP ambassador status. And that's exactly what happened! A VIP brand ambassador played a pivotal role in spreading the message and tools of the book, reaching a diverse audience ranging from stay-at-home parents to entrepreneurs to CEOs. The role offered exclusive perks, including the chance to collaborate with Daymond John and his team, access to an exclusive online community, specially curated content, and participation in an ambassador-only webinar hosted by Daymond John. This position allowed individuals to contribute to making a positive impact in the lives of many while enjoying unique networking and learning opportunities.

"I'll have the team send you an email." He thanked me for offering to help support the book launch, we shook hands, and I was officially in.

I walked out of that room with a $25,000 check, an invaluable mentoring session during which I learned so much, and a brand-new venture as a VIP ambassador that at minimum secured me a one-year relationship with Daymond John. A full year of communication during which another opportunity could potentially present itself, an opportunity I wouldn't have otherwise known about.

At the end of that day, as my then-husband and I dined at a great New York restaurant to celebrate such a wonderful achievement, I felt like I had finally made it. After years of peer pressure, of feeling like I was less than everybody else around me because they had what I didn't or couldn't have, I felt like I was no longer keeping up with the Joneses. I *was* a Jones, and now people had to keep up with me.

As much as I wish I could tell you that I have been a Jones ever since, this is not where my story ends. Not even close. One week to the day that I met Daymond John, my entire world collapsed around me. Remember what you read in the introduction? That's exactly what happened. Because I had won the Bob Evans grant, I was scheduled to be a guest on many podcasts, do countless interviews, and so much more. So, every time I had to speak in a microphone or be on camera, I put on my best business attire, showcased a bright smile, and spoke about how lucky and blessed I was. That's what people saw on the outside. And when they see a smiling woman who looks like she has it all together, they don't question what's really going on behind closed doors. They don't even think that, at the end of this interview, you're going back to an empty apartment and sleeping on a cot. After all, who would possibly believe that this woman, who's just been given a whole lot of money to grow her company and who's been mentored by one of the most brilliant businessmen in the country, is falling apart and feels like a fraud because of it?

It was one of the hardest lessons I have ever had to learn: What you see on the outside doesn't always match what it is on the inside. In the years that followed, I began seeing some of the companies that I looked up to, that I wanted Mutt's Sauce to become like, collapse and close down shop. *They were doing so well,* I thought. But did I actually know how they were doing? Not at all. Based on their social media posts and the way their CEOs spoke in interviews, they seemed to be skyrocketing and that there was no stopping them. These were some of the same companies that I had tried so hard to emulate. I mean, these were the Joneses I had been trying to keep up with. I guess we had all fallen to peer pressure.

SECRET SAUCE: How can entrepreneurs not fall to peer pressure?

Know and believe that what is meant for you will come at the time it is meant to. I wanted to pitch Daymond John four years prior to that one-on-one mentoring session in New York. For four years, I couldn't stop thinking that I had failed on *Shark Tank* when I did not get the investment I was hoping to get. Looking back on it now, I see that it all happened when it was supposed to.

Also for years, I had tried hard to become a mother and cried myself to sleep when doctors couldn't help me any longer. Then, in 2020, God blessed me with a beautiful, healthy, and happy baby boy. If I could go back and tell my younger self something, it would be: Stop trying to emulate others because you don't know what they are actually going through, so keep your eyes on your path. Trying to be what others are will only distract you from your goals.

Peer pressure presents a familiar hurdle on the entrepreneurial voyage, nudging us toward imitation and steering us from our authentic path. To safeguard your journey and purpose, internalize the notion that destined opportunities materialize in their own time. Here's my advice to gracefully navigate peer pressure while fostering your distinctiveness:

Embrace divine timing. Firmly trust that your achievements will unfold when the time is right. Comparing your odyssey to others can breed unwarranted stress and self-doubt. Patience becomes your trusted companion as you persevere in your pursuits.

Reshape setbacks as stepping stones. Each setback propels you forward to eventual triumph. Even experiences that might seem like failures contribute to your evolution. Have faith that they're integral segments of your unique trajectory.

Celebrate your individuality. Recognize that your expedition diverges from others'. Celebrate your strengths, experiences, and insights. Rather than replicating their routes, channel your energy into shaping your distinctive course.

Cultivate resilience amid challenges. The path is laden with challenges, forging your mettle in the crucible of experience. As you've overcome personal trials, bolster your resolve against external pressures.

Define success on your terms. Success eludes a universal template. Shape your definition based on your aspirations, principles, and passions. Refuse to allow external benchmarks to shape your self-worth.

Draw inspiration, not replication. Look up to mentors and achievers for inspiration, not for cloning. Immerse yourself in their stories, adapting their insights to your unique context as you weave them into your narrative.

Engage in self-discovery for self-actualization. Dedicate time to unearth your strengths, vulnerabilities, and aspirations. This self-awareness fuels decisions aligned with your true self and it propels you toward self-actualization.

Prioritize holistic well-being. Remember, the journey resembles a marathon, not a sprint. Prioritize self-care and balance between work and life. Guard against both burnout and the high cost of meeting societal expectations.

Cultivate a supportive circle. Surround yourself with kindred spirits who value your path and endorse your uniqueness. Lean on this network when confronted with external pressures.

Embrace patience, gratitude, and personal journey. Acknowledge each stride forward, regardless of its magnitude. Cultivate gratitude for your steps and practice patience as you journey toward your goals. Remember, the one thing that truly sets you apart as an entrepreneur is your life journey.

Your voyage to authenticity is your most potent asset. Revel in the ebb and flow of your journey, a singular route crafted exclusively for you. Reject conformity and embrace your true self; in doing so, you'll discover that triumph, fulfillment, and growth unfurl organically, eliminating the need for comparison or mimicry. Your expedition serves as a manifestation of your individuality, and therein lies your unparalleled strength.

PART III:
ROCK BOTTOM
IS FINANCIAL

CHAPTER NINE

ROCK BOTTOM IS FINANCIAL LITERACY

"I'm trying to keep up with you!" my mentee told me as we were sitting in front of each other. "You are doing so well in business and life, and I am striving to be just like you."

Yep, I'm a Jones.

I should have been flattered by her words. I should have felt like this moment brought me back full circle to when I was the one listening to my mentor on how to scale my business and get to the next level. I should have felt proud of everything I had achieved.

But I didn't. I couldn't.

The persona I showed the world and the human being behind it were two different individuals. All she saw was Charlynda Scales, winner of the Bob Evans grant, second runner-up at Ms. Veteran America, mentored by Daymond John, photographed at every military ball while wearing the most beautiful gowns. What she didn't see was Charlynda Scales, drowning in debt, living in an empty apartment, sleeping on a cot, having no clue where to get the money to keep paying her divorce lawyer's fees. In addition, Mutt's Sauce was barely making enough sales at one point to cover operating costs.

I'm an imposter, I thought, as images of how I got to that point flashed before my eyes.

"Do you know that I had to shut down FUBU four times?" Daymond John had revealed in one of his own interviews. "Because I used the funds in all the wrong ways," he said. "I can tell you how to quickly and efficiently blow a million dollars."

"How did you do that?" I asked him during our one-on-one mentoring session.

"I bought cars and just about anything else I didn't need," he said, looking at me and shaking his head. "I spent money on stuff. Stuff. And as a result, I didn't have any money to keep the business afloat, so I had to shut it down."

I was speechless.

"Don't make my same mistake. It's going to be tempting, but you have to resist the temptation."

Remembering his words, I thought I'd always be able to resist temptation.

I really believed I would. After all, I had spent years in the military and thought of myself as a highly disciplined person. And at first, I was very disciplined. In fact, I spent most of the $25,000 from Bob Evans on inventory. But, as you know, things in my personal life unraveled. And that's when my financial literacy, my discipline, and my mental health went flying out of the window.

I couldn't stand being at my empty apartment, faced with the absolute nothing that my life had become. The apartment was as empty as I felt inside. I had invested so much into my relationship, which had then gone up in flames. I couldn't handle the loneliness. So, I began distracting myself by filling up my schedule: I signed up to attend every possible military ball and every possible conference. I spent money on gowns, plane tickets, conference fees, and so much more. I was being photographed at every event that mattered. At one point, I had to have another foot surgery, but I didn't let that stop me from flying to Miami soon after and attending Grant Cardone's 10X Growth Conference with a boot on my foot. I remember passing a line of over 500 anxious fans, waiting to get their books signed by Daymond John. I had a conference employee push me to the front so I could at least say hi to him. The shock on Daymond's face had me in stitches. "What happened?!" His eyes were wide, as he instructed the employee to wheel me to where his team was sitting. "Long story," I replied as I hobbled out of the chair. Before any more words could be said, the crowd started screaming. Behind us was Grant Cardone, walking up to Daymond and I to surprise everyone in line. He greeted Daymond and turned to me saying, "What happened?!" With all the hype of the moment, all I could mutter was, "I was kicking so much ass!"

"Did y'all hear that!? She was kicking ass! 10X! Let's go!" Cue the three of us taking a photo, and end scene.

"You are such an inspiration," one of the attendees told me when she saw me afterward in the wheelchair. "You are committed to not let anything stop you from achieving your goals."

Actually, I'm here because the alternative—being at the apartment recovering from surgery—would have pushed me over the edge and even further into depression, I wanted to say. Instead, I smiled.

Soon, bills began to pile up. Now that I had increased inventory, I needed a bigger warehouse to store all of it. I also needed more money for marketing. In my private life, other bills were starting to become significant and I could no longer keep up with my lifestyle. The rent alone on my empty apartment was $2,200 a month. I was clearly living well beyond my means, which was exactly what Daymond John had told me not to do.

I can't believe it. I fell for it.

Difficult times called for difficult measures. So, I left my job, moved to Ohio, and cut back on business expenses. But at the same time, my parents moved in with me and soon after my assistant followed when her marriage unexpectedly fell apart, too. I couldn't turn any of my permanent houseguests away, though. Being an only child, I have always felt responsible for my parents. *It is not only an honor, but my duty to take care of them, because they raised me.* Then, I couldn't turn away my assistant, because she had single-handedly saved my business from going even deeper into debt and had also given me a place to stay when I had nowhere else to go. I felt a deep sense of obligation to help her get her life back together.

But my bills kept piling up, and my job as a bartender was not paying me well enough to keep up with them. In a desperate attempt to solve the situation, I took out loans. Unfortunately, I soon found out that was the worst thing I could have done because a loan is something you have to pay back—often with high interests. So, instead of decreasing my debt, loans increased it because now I owed money to the bank and the interest kept accumulating the longer it took me to pay it back.

I was drowning.

Two years had gone by since I had won the Bob Evans grant and I found myself more depressed than ever. *What did I do to myself?* It was time to ask myself the hard questions. Slowly, I came to the understanding that the reason why I had gone all out and spent so much on *stuff*—as Daymond John called it—instead of applying everything I had learned about discipline and allow my business to take off, was because I was unhappy. Going to yet another conference, dressing up for yet another military ball, being surrounded by other successful entrepreneurs who finally saw me as one of them because of my accolades, provided me with a high that I craved.

But the high was temporary. It began and ended with the ball, the conference, the get-together. When I went back to the empty apartment, I still cried myself to sleep on that lonely cot. Clearly, happiness was not to be found outside in the world. Happiness was an inside job. Though it took me longer than I would like to admit, I was finally able to pull up my sleeves and begin working on two main things: making peace with myself to find happiness within and repaying my debt. That's how I was able to turn this rock bottom into a trampoline.

SECRET SAUCE: How can entrepreneurs become financially literate to avoid falling into debt or succeed in recovering from it?

Know your numbers. One thing I did when I was sinking deeper and deeper in debt was to not check my balance. I did not log into my bank account because I couldn't stand facing the numbers. That is, until I understood there was no reason not to do so—not if I wanted to finally begin fixing the issue. Avoidance is never the answer because it will never make the problem go away. By avoiding it, the problem will not only stay there, but in many cases, it will also grow bigger. Once I finally logged into my bank account and looked at the numbers, I knew exactly what I was dealing with. I checked every single expense and began studying ways to limit them. And I did so on a weekly basis, making it part of my routine.

Apply for grants. I soon learned that the loans I had taken out to help my business were now actually hurting it because of the interest rate. That's when I realized that the way to go about getting financial help for a growing business was not through loans, but through grants. With a grant, I wouldn't have to pay them back. It was basically free money. A Google search helped me narrow down the grants I was eligible for: food industry, small business, veteran-owned, and so on. Though for some of them I had missed the deadline, I still looked at the application process and studied the questions asked. After reading through a few of them, I realized that many of the questions on several grant applications were quite similar. So, I opened a new document on my monitor and created a spreadsheet with a list of questions copied and pasted from these applications. Determined to apply for as many grants as possible, and to do so in an organized and timely manner, I made time to answer every question carefully. I even wrote down a long and a short version of most answers because I noticed that some grants asked for a more detailed explanation while others wanted the short and sweet one. Aside from writing down the answers, I also made several videos of different lengths (one minute, five minutes, and so on) in which I introduced the company, explained why I needed the grant, and talked about how I would use the funds. A fancy camera wasn't needed. A phone camera worked just fine.

One of the most important things I wrote down was when each grant opened and closed the application process—thus crafting a calendar of sorts. It took me time to create all this content, but when it came time for me to apply for these grants, I was ready. In most cases, all I had to do was copy and paste my answers or slightly adapt them to fit the question better. Soon, I found myself applying for at least one grant a month and I was doing so in an organized and disciplined way. Though grants worked well for me, they are not the only source of income when needing that little boost to fund your business without having to take a loan. Pitch contests, crowdfunding campaigns, and fundraisers are also excellent ways to help your business because, just like grants, you don't have to pay them back—and as such, they won't negatively contribute to your debt. If you have family and friends who support you and your business endeavor, you can also invite them to contribute to your business growth.

Ask yourself important questions. Of course, the ideal scenario would be to avoid falling into debt altogether. However, whether you fell into debt or not, it is crucial to be aware of your costs and earnings. So, ask yourself these important questions: How much does it cost to provide the service you provide? How much does it cost to produce your product? How much does it cost you to operate your business? What are your margins? But above all, you need to know what problem you are solving. After all, this is what people want to know: Is your service helping me save money? How is your product going to improve my life? The answers to these questions will provide you with a clear vision that will help you handle—or, best-case scenario, avoid—financial hardships along the way.

Save money. Aside from finding ways to make money, it is also crucial to look for ways to save money. Many product-based businesses use an out-of-state manufacturer, but I decided to look for one closer to me and I happened to find one nearby. After I switched manufacturers, I was not only able to cut costs (shipping fees had me bleeding money for the longest time), but I also saved time because it didn't take weeks for my product to arrive at the destination since the manufacturer was geographically close to me. This turned out to be a win-win situation because I was also helping the community by investing in it. I recommend you do the same: Look for businesses within your own community to see if there is anyone you could hire or collaborate with to save you money on production costs.

Take part in conferences. I know that what I described in my story can be taken as a lesson not to go to conferences. But it is crucial that entrepreneurs be surrounded by other entrepreneurs to learn from them, to connect with them, and to network. How are you going to operate a company earning six or seven figures if you have not been around people doing the same or more? There is a lot to learn from those who've been there and done that. My advice would be not to attend every single one of them—like I did when I needed to distract myself from my crumbling private life. Instead, do your homework: Which conferences are going to be the most beneficial to you and your business? Once you have that list, calculate the costs associated with each one of them. Will it fit within your yearly budget? If so, be sure to set that money aside: Set a budget and stick to it. If you don't have the necessary funds to attend all the conferences on your list, take one or two off and set a personal goal to perhaps attend them a year later than you wanted to. Whatever you do, don't go over the budget, or you'll find yourself drowning in debt, just like I did.

Don't mix personal and business money. During my one-on-one mentoring session with Daymond John, he asked me how I had been able to fund Mutt's Sauce up until that point.

"Well, I used all the money I had saved up while I was on active duty," I said. "I always said that if I ever were to be promoted to major, I was going to take my savings, which amounted to $25,000, go to the BMW dealership, and pay for a brand-new car with the cash, right off the lot."

"Instead, you took that money and invested in your company," he said.

I nodded yes.

"But you still want the BMW," he said.

I nodded again.

"Now that Bob Evans is giving you the money you had planned on using to buy the car of your dreams, don't you dare use it for personal reasons," he warned me. "That is the fastest way to fail. I guarantee you that. I know it from personal experience."

I promised him I wouldn't. And I didn't, though as you have seen, I eventually did fall into the trap of spending money for personal reasons even though it was always meant to be spent for Mutt's Sauce.

It takes a high level of discipline not to fall into the temptation of rewarding yourself. I remember a fellow veteran telling me he had won a $50,000 grant and spent $10,000 on a Disney World trip with his children. "I had never been able to take them there, so I decided to finally do it." But now he had $10,000 less to invest in his business because of it. Did it feel good at the time when he was having fun on vacation? Of course, it did! But he soon found himself even more stressed out because the cash he had planned on using to grow his business wasn't all there anymore. Another fellow entrepreneur told me he had used all the money given to him after he won a pitch contest to pay off personal debt. But that's not what the money was given to him for, so his business suffered because of it. Though he had reduced his personal debt, he had not been able to scale the company the way he wanted to. Indeed, it's not easy to resist the temptation. But if you succeed in doing so, you will be grateful you did.

Hire what you suck at. Entrepreneurship can often feel like a lonely journey, but it doesn't have to be that way. Wearing multiple hats (CEO, CFO, CMO, and so on) can be exhausting, to say the least. You are never going to be able to master every single role when it comes to running a business. You might be a very skilled networker, but you lack financial knowledge. You might be a skilled accountant, but you lack marketing knowledge. Though you still need to understand how every aspect of your company works to make sure everything is running smoothly and under control, don't forget to ask for help. Or, as I call it, hire what you suck at. Suck at social media? Hire a social media expert to run the platforms for you. Suck at running numbers? Hire an accountant who can do that for you. But don't forget to check your budget, of course, and see if you can afford to hire someone to help you in that specific aspect of your business. Also, keep in mind that if you can't hire an expert because your budget doesn't allow it at the moment, you can always look for interns. College students would be more than happy to become an intern for your company and gain hands-on experience and a nice, shiny letter of recommendation they can present to their future employer.

Get a Board of Advisors. The phenomenon called "founder's syndrome" is when one person has so much power and influence over company decisions that it can be almost destructive. A remedy for this is to make sure the founder, especially solopreneurs, have a sounding board and accountability process in place. Mutt's Sauce has had several mentors over the years, but only one board of advisors. In looking for a board, you want to target people in a similar way to hiring what you suck at. These professionals are skilled in areas in which you are lacking. For me, it was sales, finances, processes, and—frankly—people who I knew would give it to me "straight with no chaser." Among them was my SCORE mentor, John Soutar; Donerik Black, a well-respected serial entrepreneur who grew up in Dayton, where Mutt's Sauce is manufactured; the late William "Bill" Cox, my advisor and fellow military veteran from the Ohio Procurement Technical Assistance Center (PTAC); and Phil Storage, a consumer-packaged goods expert. In my phone I have him listed as "Phil the FOOD GOD" because he was instrumental in launching brands like Ken's Foods and Sweet

Baby Ray's barbecue sauce. Unbeknownst to me, I was a guest speaker at the college his son attended. "My dad knows about food business and could probably help you"—was the biggest understatement.

The point is, you need to surround yourself with people with the same values who are smarter than you. Phil was patient and methodical. Donerik would drop several f-bombs—our meetings were more terrifying than going on *Shark Tank*—but you'd walk away feeling fantastic. Bill understood government contracts, but we talked mostly about self-care. I even re-connected with previous advisors like Wendy Vloedman, who was a lead facilitator at a course I graduated from at Aileron, The Course for Presidents. She was kind and practical. Wendy was masterful with the art of the follow-up, a skill I adopted from her that paid dividends through the years.

Be teachable. Now a mentor and teacher, I have learned one annoying thing about my industry. It's a more enjoyable experience when the entrepreneur acts on your advice. Time is the most precious asset we have. To ask for someone's time is to take time away from their mission, their families, and their time off. Don't waste it. If you have a board of advisors, come prepared to give them a thorough and transparent update. Have your numbers ready. Don't hide anything. People can't advise you properly if they don't know the whole truth. Mentors typically care more about the whole person—your personal life included—than a business advisor. Adjust accordingly but show up prepared.

Be disciplined. This is the most important secret sauce of all. Discipline is what is going to make your business succeed. Every single piece of advice that I have provided you with in this section comes down to being disciplined. Being disciplined is the hardest thing to do because there will be temptations along the way that will make you brush off impending consequences with, "Oh well, I'll cross that bridge when I get to it. For now, I deserve to enjoy life." And of course you do! We all deserve to enjoy our life. But when the cost poses a serious threat to the success, longevity, and sustainability of your business, it stops being a matter of enjoyment and starts being a matter of self-destruction. After all the mistakes I made with my finances, I came to the understanding that if I wanted Mutt's Sauce to turn into a multigenerational business that could provide wealth not only to me, but also my child, and his children, I needed to change my mindset. I am the reason why Mutt's Sauce fails. I am the reason why Mutt's Sauce succeeds. I am the one who chooses which way it will go.

I choose to do the work now, so I can reap my personal definition of success later on. You can, too.

CHAPTER TEN

ROCK BOTTOM IS A BUSINESS PARTNER

"Have you made a decision on whether or not you are going to the Military Influencer Conference this year?" my assistant asked me as she sorted through papers that had been piling up on my desk for weeks.

"Oh, is it that time of year again?" I said, pouring myself a cup of coffee. "Man, I feel like we just came back from the last one."

"It's not time to go just yet," she said, shaking her head as she took a quick look at the papers. "Charlynda, some of these are past due and some others have not even been filed yet. I know you've been going through a lot, but this is not the time to fall back on important financial documents." She grabbed a bunch of them and waved them at me. "You know what, I am just going to take them with me and figure it out."

"Thank you," I whispered, looking down at the cup of coffee, the beverage so hot it was steaming out of the mug, making me feel like I was getting a facial. At this point, I didn't know the difference between a neurodivergent brain and a neurotypical brain, but we were definitely polar opposites. Sometimes I'm focused, and sometimes my brain operates as orderly as Fraggle Rock hair.

"Anyway, going back to the conference," she said, as she started making two different piles of papers on my desk—

though I didn't know what the label for each pile was. *Perhaps "Past Due" and "Not Filed,"* I thought. "As I was saying, it's not time to go there just yet, but they're having their early bird sale and it's more convenient if we buy tickets now rather than later. They're offering a great discount."

"OK, sounds good," I said, sitting on the couch, still holding on to my cup of coffee, not yet ready to take the first sip.

"So, you're going?" she asked, finally taking a break from the papers and looking at me.

I nodded yes.

"Alright, I'll take care of the tickets then," she said. "Do you plan on being a vendor, applying as a speaker, or just a guest?"

I sighed. Heavily.

I didn't know what to answer. These were simple questions, ones that an entrepreneur should be able to answer without any hesitation. But I was having a hard time thinking about my business, my career, and my future as an entrepreneur because I was in a funk.

Thank God I have you, I thought to myself as I looked at my assistant. Lately, she had been spending more time at my house trying to sort my life out than at her own place. After living with her for a while, I had finally found a place to call my own. However, finding a house and making it a home were two completely different things. Though it wasn't as bad as when I had to rent the empty apartment in D.C. and sleep on a cot, I also wasn't ready to make my new humble abode into a home. I just didn't know where to even begin. The chaos I felt inside had also quickly translated into my outside world, as the pile of papers proved.

"I think you should be a vendor," she said, shaking me out of my daze.

"Alright, sure," I said.

"I'm going to bring these documents home," she said, as she grabbed her purse that had been sitting on the chair by the desk. "By the way, I brought you some dinner. It's in the fridge, you'll just need to warm it up for a minute or two in the microwave."

I was speechless. I was so thankful for her. She had been handling so much on her own, giving me space and time to pull myself together. She never complained about the many responsibilities she certainly did not know were going to be handed to her when she accepted the job. Heck, when I hired her, not even I knew this was where we would end up.

I smiled at her and thanked her before she left the house.

A few days later, she came back and handed me a well-thought-out plan of action.

"This year's conference will be in Orlando," she said as she explained each point of the plan. "So, I booked you a room with two queen beds—it was cheaper than the one with a king bed—at the same hotel the conference takes place. Also, continental breakfast is included, so be sure not to skip it because you'll need the energy to network. Any questions so far?"

I shook my head and let her continue.

"I have already hired a couple of people to run the booth for you because I don't want you to have to stand by it all day," she said, pointing at the names of the new hires on the sheet of paper I had in my hands. "Also, I have sent an order to the local printing store, so we have enough flyers, brochures, and everything else we need for the booth. They will be ready by the end of the week."

"Thank you," I said.

"I stayed within the budget, and actually cut a few unnecessary expenses so we've saved some money," she said. "Basically, all you need to do to attend this event is get to the airport on time—which I'm going to make sure of because

I'm going, too—and show up to do what you do best. You don't have to worry about anything else because I've taken care of it all. The last thing I need to do is to take the gowns or whatever other outfit you plan on wearing there to the dry cleaners. But don't worry about that for now because we have some time to figure that out. I just wanted to make sure the conference ticket, hotel, and flight were booked well in advance."

"I don't know what I would do without you," I told her.

"Me neither," she said. We both started laughing.

I needed that. It was in that moment that I realized I couldn't remember when the last time was that I had laughed so genuinely.

As time went by, she became more and more invaluable to me, prompting me to make an important decision.

"Would you consider becoming a partner in Mutt's Sauce?" I asked her one day.

"What?" she said, clearly caught off guard.

"We work very well together, and you know Mutt's Sauce inside out, especially because you've been helping me for the past two years," I explained. "Let's be honest, you've been running this business almost completely on your own for the past few weeks and you've managed to juggle even what I'm supposed to take care of. Making you a partner seems to be the most obvious choice."

"But what about your family?" she said, "wouldn't they be upset if you made me a partner instead of them? I mean, I have no ties to Mutt's Sauce, whereas your relatives are part of Mutt's family."

"If there's one thing I've learned from my mentors, it's that you should never work with family in that manner. It will change the relationship because at some point, you'll have to face problems, and these problems can bring animosity among family members, which can lead to relationships being changed forever, and not for the better," I said. "That's why we have been hiring them as independent contractors as opposed to full-time employees or even partners. I don't want anything to compromise my relationship with any of my family members. I love them. These are people I plan on having in my life forever, and I don't ever want business to interfere and ruin what we have."

"Oh, but you'd be OK if business were to interfere and ruin what *we* have?" she joked, soliciting another laughter from both. "But you know I don't want to be in the spotlight and don't do well when it comes to networking. I'm not like you. You shine when you're among people, while I'd be a shy and quiet mess."

"But that's exactly why I want you as a partner," I said, immediately realizing that my words could have been easily misinterpreted. "I mean—"

I didn't have to explain myself because she laughed out so hard, she almost cried.

"I mean, we are great at two different things, so we complement each other," I said. "Your strengths reside in the tactical part of the business—planning, scheduling, coordinating, and so on. Mine instead reside in the strategy of the company—networking, socializing, making deals and so forth. Together, we make a great team."

"I appreciate that, but how would we even begin formalizing a partnership?" Her questions made me understand she was actually considering the option, which made me smile.

"I looked into it, and we would have to do a sweat equity deal," I explained. I had been thinking about making her this offer for a while. These decisions are so important and cannot be taken lightly. I had always been a *solopreneur*, meaning I had always run the business on my own, so taking the step toward forming a partnership with someone else was not something I simply woke up one day and chose to do. The gleam in her eyes told me she was going to seriously consider my offer, and I expected to receive a positive answer from her soon after that conversation.

What happened, however, was something that I could not have predicted. She eventually left the company and moved away. It wasn't because of the company. After helping me through my divorce, allowing me time to grieve the dissolution of the life I thought I had, and carrying Mutt's Sauce through the tough times, her own private life had come crumbling down all around her. So, she made the difficult decision to move out of state and leave her job. Though I completely understood the many reasons why she had decided to make the move—I had just been in her shoes—I couldn't help but feel like I had just hit rock bottom. The partner I had counted on for so many years had left. *Am I going to be able to run it all on my own?* That question scared me straight because I hadn't been a solopreneur for the past two years. Sure, on paper nothing had ever changed because she and I never actually got to the point of signing any contract that bonded us into a *de jure* partnership. But we were certainly *de facto* partners. I knew that going ahead without her was going to be difficult, to say the least. However, I had no other choice. I pulled up my sleeves and made it happen. Though there were bumps in the road, she had done such a wonderful job at organizing my files and keeping track of every expense and contract that it was not as hard as I thought it was going to be to fill in for both roles. Soon, it became part of my routine to tackle what she used to, and Mutt's Sauce lived to see another day.

SECRET SAUCE: How can entrepreneurs avoid entering a business partnership with the wrong person?

Though I was able to turn that rock bottom into a trampoline, I am aware that history is filled with many partnerships that have gone up into flames, most of them resulting in the complete derailment or even total failure of the business venture. As entrepreneurs, it is crucial to consider several things when it comes to choosing the right partner.

Court your partner. I know this recommendation sounds like it doesn't belong in this book but humor me. When it comes to any great relationship that will last the test of time, it is important that you don't take courting your business partner for granted. Of course, I don't mean it in the romantic sense of the word. I mean courting in the sense that it would be the only way to truly get to know the person with whom you intend to get into a business venture. Go out to dinner together, talk about mundane things as well as more important topics and see if your values align. Get to know them well enough so you can see who they are and how they behave when around family, friends, and coworkers. My assistant saw me at my worst, and I admired her strength and dedication not only to Mutt's Sauce but also to taking care of me, reminding me what I was capable of, telling me when it was time to put my big girl pants back on because we had a business to run, and cheering me on as I networked our way to success. She was truly a like-hearted person. As explained before, a like-hearted person is going to have the same core values as you, while a like-minded person is going to have the same goals. While my assistant and I did not see eye to eye on many things, and our personalities could not have been more different, we were like-hearted. This was the secret to our great relationship, that we both cared about and valued the same things. Getting in business with a like-hearted person will also allow you to understand, and potentially predict, how they would behave in difficult situations—and trust me, there will be many, regardless of how successful the business is going to be.

Ask the tough questions. Before entering a partnership, you and your partner must sit down and ask yourselves tough questions, because the answers will have to be clearly written in the contract to avoid any litigations or misunderstandings later on—especially should one of the following scenarios present itself. For example, what are you going to do if your partner gets sick? Of course, I don't mean just a bad summer cold. I mean a real illness that, for whatever reason, forces your partner to take a significant step back, even a hiatus, from the business while they recover. You have to make sure that there are going to be clear steps in place that you can follow.

What if your partner dies? Are you going to set up a life insurance policy for both you and your partner should the unthinkable happen? A life insurance policy could help you gain that financial breathing room while you figure out the future of your company as you grieve the loss.

What if your partner were to develop an addiction? What terms would have to be in place that would force your partner out of the company? These two questions deal with one of the most important words: accountability. Times are going to get tough and when they do, people react differently. Some try to self-medicate by turning to alcohol, for example. What if the temporary lapse turns into a serious addiction? You need to ensure that the business doesn't suffer because of it, which means that you or your partner are going to be held accountable for your actions, since you both have skin in the game. What if your partner comments on a social media post and attracts so much backlash that is now a threat to your business? These are just some of the many questions you should ask one another. That's why it's important to truly get to know the person you intend to embark upon an entrepreneurial journey with. It might cost you your business if you don't.

Grow together. In business, just like in life, there is always something new to learn and there are opportunities to grow. Be sure to attend conferences, leadership lessons, and courses with your partner so you can both grow together as professionals. Being on the same page, also when it comes to entrepreneurial growth, is important because it ensures that there are no gaps between you and your partner. If you're anything like me, it is not easy for you to trust people. But when it comes to working together with another person, you will have to take that leap of faith over and over again and trust that the person you're running the business with knows what they are doing and will not put the company in jeopardy. Hopefully, the more you grow together, the more you will trust one another.

Don't reinvent the wheel. When my assistant left, I had no idea how I was going to run the company on my own. Fortunately for me, she had left plenty of templates to follow because she was a big believer of "don't reinvent the wheel." For example, she made templates for us to use every time we needed to hire a contractor, so we wouldn't have to spend (better yet, waste) time writing down the same hiring documents and forms. Having a clear system in place for me to follow was what eventually allowed me to go on after she no longer worked for and with me. Be sure that you and your partner develop a well-organized system to follow should one of you no longer be able to work. It can save your company's future.

Different skills. As detailed in the opening story, my assistant was very good at what I suck at. She was methodical and organized, but also introverted and shy in social situations. She and I excelled at different things, which is what made our partnership that much more valuable and successful. When it comes to choosing a partner, aside from ensuring that you are like-hearted, you also have to understand where their strengths and weaknesses lie. If you are both excellent at seeing the bigger picture, you are both going to fail when it comes to getting down to the nitty gritty of things. However, if you excel at different things, you will have a balanced team.

Communicate. This seems like a given, but it is one of the hardest things to do when it comes to any relationship. Open communication is key. It's easy to talk to one another when things are going well, sales are skyrocketing, and business is booming. But what about when things start going sour? What if your partner says something or does something that hurts your feelings or hurts the business? That's when it's easy to forget that communication is key. People who tend to shy away from confrontation are also those who prefer to sweep things under the rug instead of facing them head-on. Guess what, the dust is going to continue to accumulate until it can no longer be overlooked. The military also taught me that bad news doesn't get better with time. That's why it's best to have conversations, especially the most uncomfortable ones, as soon as the situation presents itself. When the line of communication is open, it's crucial to be as honest as possible. Sugarcoating things because you're worried about hurting people's feelings can often lead to misunderstandings, which then leads to the problem being left unresolved. Of course, don't be rude either, because then you will have to face a whole other set of problems that pose a serious threat to the survival of the business.

Choose wisely. Choosing a business partner is not something that should ever be done lightly because it can be the difference between the success or failure of your business. Keeping all these suggestions in mind will hopefully help you in making the right decision. And remember that, if you are not 100 percent convinced that you have met the right business partner yet, you can still rely on the one person who, though they might have let you down from time to time, is still waking up every single day with the scope of working hard to pursue the entrepreneurial dream: yourself.

CHAPTER ELEVEN

ROCK BOTTOM IS TAKING THE LEAP

T hree minutes is a very short time. Three minutes is a very long time. It depends on what you are doing during these three minutes. When I was at a conference, networking among peers, learning from them, and promoting Mutt's Sauce, three minutes flew by. When I was waiting for the pregnancy test to reveal if I was pregnant, three minutes was an eternity.

Please, please be positive. I prayed silently.

I had been down this road so many times before. For the entire five years of my marriage I tried so hard to become a mother. Countless checkups, specialists, second opinions, super painful treatments. Nothing worked. And people still asked, "You've been married for some time now, when are you going to have a baby?" Cue my automatic reply, "We're working on it." Always accompanied by a smile. A fake smile, because all I really wanted to say was, "I have been trying and trying and I still have no baby to hold. Every time the pregnancy test turns negative, I cry so many tears that I fold over in pain. Am I not supposed to be a mother? And if I'm not supposed to be a mother, then what is my life's purpose?" I remember telling him when we met that I wanted to be a mother at twenty-five. I was twenty-three at the time. Although our marriage was five years, we courted for over a decade. I deserved to be a mother. But with every attempt to get pregnant, motherhood slipped farther and farther away from me.

Two minutes.

Now, as a single woman, I had made the decision to try to become a mother once again. The doctors had told me that I had every odd stacked up against me: my age, previous failed attempts, several health issues, and so much more.

"Listen, this is it," my doctor told me. "There is going to be nothing else we can do if this doesn't work out. Falling in love can happen at any age, but your womb has an expiration date." She had a great point. Also, I knew plenty of emotionally and mentally messed up adults who came from toxic, two-parent homes. It was no longer the status symbol it used to be.

I had to try. Just one more time. *Either it works, or I will have to make peace with the fact that I was destined not to carry my own child.* How would I go about making peace with infertility though, I had no idea.

One minute.

I paced the bathroom back and forth like a caged animal, forcing myself to not even peek at the pregnancy test set by the sink.

"What am I doing?" I whispered to myself. "What if it's positive?" I wasn't even supposed to do this. The doctor clearly said to wait on her phone call with the results of my blood test.

This was certainly not the right time to have a baby. The ink on my divorce papers was barely dry, my bank accounts were suffering because of the increasing debt, and my parents had just moved in with me. *I don't even have a room to use as a nursery.* The other extra room I had was currently occupied by my assistant, who had also moved in with me to escape her own personal struggles. I had a house full of permanent guests and nowhere to put a crib. Not to mention, my jam-packed schedule. I had so much going on with Mutt's Sauce and a calendar full of events to attend, which obviously involved a lot of traveling. I was scheduled to be a speaker at a few conferences across the country. Cue the crazy and irrational thoughts: *Am I going to be able to stay in my business suits if I get pregnant? Or will I have to buy a whole new wardrobe? What if the pregnancy brings complications and I have to be on bed rest? Is the business going to suffer because of the setbacks?* So much self-doubt that I started feeling like the bathroom was way too small and I didn't have enough room to breathe.

Beep, beep, beep.

The timer on my phone, the one that had been counting down the 180 seconds it took for the pregnancy test to reveal whether or not I was going to be a mother, plus extra time to satiate my anxiety, had gone off. My hands were shaking so badly that I dropped the phone to the floor as I tried to stop the beeping. I closed my eyes and took a deep breath in.

This is it, Charlynda.

I put both hands on the counter as if needing to grab on to something because either result was going to be life changing. I slowly opened my eyes and traveled with my gaze from my fingertips all the way to the white stick of the pregnancy test. Since I didn't want to spend time staring at a potentially faded second line wondering if I was pregnant or not—I wasn't particularly fond of those tests because that second line can often be so faded that you can't even see it—I had decided to go with the clearer one that simply stated: Pregnant/Not Pregnant. I needed the test to be straightforward. No guessing game involved.

As my eyes made their way up to the small rectangular screen on the stick, I bit my bottom lip hard, though I couldn't feel any pain. My heart was about to jump out of my throat.

I blinked.

The first few letters appeared.

I blinked again.

There was something missing.

Oh my God . . .

I lowered myself toward the screen to make sure my sight was not deceiving me.

Pregnant.

There was no Not in front of it.

It said Pregnant.

I'm pregnant . . .

I gasped.

"I'm pregnant!"

It finally happened. I was going to be a mother. I grabbed the pregnancy test and rushed out of the bathroom, looking for my mother. I knew she had been praying hard for me to finally experience motherhood and her reaction to the news was even more beautiful than I expected. She gave me the sweetest embrace and we both cried together, as we had done so many times before when I called her to tell her what the pregnancy test revealed. Or better, did not reveal. This time, however, those were finally tears of joy.

"You're going to be the best mother," she whispered in my ear as she caressed my hair.

As weeks went by, doctors found a 14cm tumor in my abdomen, but fortunately it did not cause any harm to the baby nor did it derail the pregnancy. Imagine that. I would've never known unless I'd taken an ultrasound, which were routine for pregnancy. Though doctors had warned me that my pregnancy was considered high risk because of several factors, God must have been looking out for me since I had a smooth and symptomless pregnancy. While I awaited my baby's arrival, my assistant decided to move out of state and quit her job at Mutt's Sauce, after I proposed to make her an official partner. Though this decision was unexpected and hardly good timing, I supported her, wrote a great recommendation letter, and resigned to a life as a single mother and solopreneur. *If other women can do it, so can I.*

Being pregnant while suddenly finding myself having to run my company on my own for the first time in two years was not easy. I often had to wear multiple hats at once, but when it happened to be just too much, I decided to scale back on duties and commitments. My baby's health and well-being were now my priority and slowing down my company for a few months had quickly become a necessity rather than a possibility.

As my due date grew closer, I took more time away from Mutt's Sauce to enjoy the last few weeks and days of my pregnancy, which I had fought so hard for, one that most doctors no longer believed possible—heck, at times, even I had lost all hope. But this baby was already so loved and so wanted. In March 2020, David Dewayne came to the world and suddenly everything made sense.

His middle name paid respect to my Uncle Dewayne. Growing up, he was someone I honestly idolized. A chef, a true professional, and one of my grandfather's five children, he was the only one who didn't have kids. Legacy is my *Why*, so I had to make sure his name lived on. The reason why I was born was now clear—to be David's mother. The reason why I had decided to not give up on my entrepreneurial dream—to leave him a tangible legacy. The reason why I had to go through so much pain and setbacks—to be able to appreciate my little miracle.

Becoming a mother when I was a single woman and while running a business that was drowning in debt was definitely not the easiest thing to do because I had to juggle so much at once. But I still took the leap because if I waited for the right time, when everything in my life felt like it was in the right place, I might never have become a mother. Fortunately, the leap I took resulted in the most positive outcome, and I do believe that had the pregnancy test been negative once again it would have had the potential of sending me down a never-ending spiral of depression. Who knows what might have happened to me and Mutt's Sauce if I didn't have my son. While the possibility of a negative outcome can be scary, in my opinion it could never be as scary as the possibility of never taking that leap. I would have much rather lived a life knowing that I had done all I could have to make my dream of motherhood happen rather than spend the rest of my days wondering what would have happened if I had tried just one last time.

Let that inspire you to take that leap into whatever it is you dream of becoming or doing.

SECRET SAUCE: How can entrepreneurs find the strength to not only take the leap but also face setbacks once they do take the leap?

When it comes to entrepreneurship, there are times when you will find yourself at a crossroads. Choosing which way to go can be the scariest thing because of the risks associated with the choice. Taking that leap can either lead you to success or failure. But in my experience, it's always better to take the leap than to regret not doing so.

Just start. When I was handed the recipe that eventually turned into Mutt's Sauce, I questioned whether or not I was indeed the best person to start this type of business. I wasn't the best cook in my family, I wasn't organized, I was quite scatterbrained. I didn't feel qualified. *Should I first learn how to cook well enough to run a business within the food* *industry? Should I get a system in place first before diving into entrepreneurship? Should I get out of active duty before starting the business that could suffer if I didn't have enough time to dedicate to it?* All these questions kept me up at night. Until I decided to just go for it and see how far I could go with it. Waiting for the perfect time to start your business is like waiting for the planets to align. You just have to go for it and figure it out along the way.

Know your audience. At Mutt's Sauce we started with two flavors: Original and Sweet N Spicy. However, while attending events and farmers' markets, many people in Ohio kept asking me when I was going to release a hot sauce version. *Good question.* So, I went right to work. Since I didn't know much—or almost anything, to be completely honest—about peppers, I took the time to study and learn about the different peppers, the flavor profile of each one, and the Scoville scale.[7] I wanted to make sure I used the right one to infuse flavor in Mutt's Sauce.

Eventually, after many trials, bottles of Benadryl (remember, I'm allergic to peppers), and countless glasses of

---

7. The Scoville scale "expresses the level of pungency or heat of a pepper based on the levels of capsaicin in a pepper. The scale was invented in 1912 by a pharmacologist named Wilbur Scoville. It involves extracting the capsaicinoids from a pepper and diluting them with a solution of sugar and water until the heat of the pepper can no longer be tasted by a panel of professionally trained taste testers. More dilutions indicate a higher heat index rating and therefore a higher concentration of capsaicinoids. The test relies on the initial amount extracted from the pepper as well as the training of the taste testers." "How Do You Measure the 'Heat' of a Pepper?" National Institute of Standards and Technology, U.S. Department of Commerce, created June 23, 2022, updated June 27, 2022, accessed August 8, 2023. https://www.nist.gov/how-do-you-measure-it/how-do-you-measure-heat-pepper#:~:text=A%20tool%2C%20called%20the%20Scoville,a%20pharmacologist%20named%20Wilbur%20Scoville.

milk to soothe the burning sensation in my mouth from trying and testing all kinds of peppers, I came to the conclusion that ghost pepper was the best one to go with. I learned that if you powder ghost pepper, it gives the sauce a nice, delayed heat to it. Soon, I took the leap and created Mutt's Sauce Ghost Pepper.

As I began selling it in Ohio, I was surprised by the overwhelmingly positive response. It was an immediate hit! So strong was the feedback received, in fact, I decided to also reach out to Spring Street Market down in my hometown of Cookeville, Tennessee. I knew the owners because my grandfather used to go there all the time. It was his favorite store. Though I did not have the capital to also expand Mutt's Sauce down in Tennessee, I thought that we could have Spring Street Market carry it and give them the exclusivity. So, I spoke to them and agreed to either go there in person to hand them documentation and invoices or send them via a fax machine—they were so old fashioned that fax machines were the most technology they had in the store, which made me fall even more in love with them. Soon after the legal paperwork had been taken care of, we had a small demonstration and called upon the local community to try out Mutt's Sauce. It was a beautiful event because so many people from my hometown came to taste the famous sauce that Mutt used to make. Given the success of the demonstration, the store decided to carry all three flavors, which was a wonderful achievement.

After a few weeks, I called the owner to see how sales were going and he told me, "Charlynda, the sauce is selling great. Except for one." *Except for one?* I asked him which one it was, and he said it was Mutt's Sauce Ghost Pepper. I couldn't believe it! Ohio had loved the new sauce, so why weren't people in Tennessee responding the same way? After thinking about it, I realized that the root of the problem might have been geographical: People down South like sweet things, while people up North prefer a bit of a bite to their food. Had I tested the Ghost Pepper sauce in Tennessee first, I probably would have decided to discontinue it because of the negative response—and possibly I would have never realized that it was a matter of palate. However, having already tested it in Ohio and having received a positive response, I was able to clearly see what the root problem was.

So, the lesson here is: Know your audience. If your product is not selling well with a specific target audience, perhaps it's not the product, but the audience. Don't be afraid to take the leap and create a new product or target another market. The worst that can happen is that, if this leap doesn't lead to the desired results, you can always look for the root problem and figure out a way to solve it.

Choose the right business model. When taking the leap of starting a business, one of the most common mistakes I have come across among entrepreneurs is choosing the wrong business model. I remember when a fellow entrepreneur I was mentoring told me how disappointed he was when his business failed.

"Why did it fail?" I asked him.

"I have no idea," he said, shrugging.

"Well, tell me what happened to the business then," I said. "Walk me through the steps you took from when you opened it until you understood it had failed."

"I wanted to open up a bakery," he began. "So, I saved the money and eventually found a brick-and-mortar place downtown where I could set up shop. I bought all the kitchen equipment and the furniture; I painted the store, decorated it, and had a grand opening where I invited all the people in the community. But soon, people stopped coming and I was never able to regain the investment I put into it."

"But why do you say it failed?" I asked him.

I could tell from his furrowed brows that he didn't understand my question.

"I don't think your business failed. I just think you chose the wrong business model."

His confusion grew.

"Instead of spending all this money on setting up a store and then seeing if customers responded positively to your cupcakes and desserts, perhaps you could have started with an e-commerce model. By baking at home, or a commercial kitchen, you could have saved a whole lot of money while at the same time testing your market. You could have promoted your business at local birthday parties or other celebrations, left business cards at events you catered for, and so on. Basically, you could have built your clientele before opening up the brick-and-mortar shop that the community did not respond well to."

"I guess you're right," he said in a low tone. "Lots of things I could have done differently. But what do I do now to fix the problem?"

"Change your business model," I said. "You took a leap and went all in with an actual store. It didn't work out, but that doesn't mean you should quit the food industry altogether. Just change the way you do business and go from there."

The more we spoke about his bakery, the more I understood why it might have failed. Aside from the business model, he also had a complicated menu to go through. It was filled with so many options that I thought, *Perhaps customers got overwhelmed and didn't know what to choose.* So, I suggested reducing the menu to a few clear dessert options.

"What are you really good at baking?" I asked him.

"I think my strength is in novelty cupcakes," he said. "Not so much on decorating them, but in the flavor combinations I propose."

"There you have it," I said. "Focus on that strength and go with it."

It was during that very conversation that he not only came up with a brand-new business model, but also a brand-new menu. However, the most important lesson he learned was that when taking a leap, things can go wrong, and you can find yourself at rock bottom, but that doesn't mean that it's the end of the road. Learn from the root problem and find a way to fix it or pivot your vision. Then, take another leap. Who knows, this one might be the trampoline that will take you to where you wanted to go in the first place.

PART IV:
ROCK BOTTOM IS UNPREDICTABLE

CHAPTER TWELVE

ROCK BOTTOM IS UNPREDICTABLE

" *M**edical experts are now beginning to use the word 'pandemic' to describe the spread of the coronavirus across the world,"* I heard the newscaster say on the television. *"We have seen terrifying images of military vehicles deployed by the Italian government that were sent to hospitals in the northern region of Lombardy. The vehicles, as previously reported, are being used to store the bodies of those who have died from the disease. Some government officials are saying that we could soon expect to see the same thing happen here in the United States of America, which of course is cause for great concern. While scientists are still looking for a cure, many of the details about the coronavirus remain unknown."*

I turned the TV off and stared at my newborn. The word "coronavirus" was everywhere you turned. There was no newspaper that didn't have it displayed in bold letters on the front page, no news station that didn't talk about it for 98 percent of their program, and no family gathering, local store, or school district where it wasn't being brought up. As talked about as it was, however, nobody seemed to know what to do about it. And how could they? A pandemic was something that was only discussed in history books, and those descriptions were usually followed by black-and-white photos of doctors wearing all-black cloaks and face masks that resembled bird beaks. This was pre-Middle Ages stuff. Certainly not things that happened in the twenty-first century! So many questions were being asked: Was this pandemic really as bad as the media was making it out to be? Was this a government conspiracy? Was this part of the biblical Armageddon?

David was born after twenty minutes of painless labor. I know, it almost seems unfair how easy the pregnancy was. My cousin Tasha, my late uncle Frankie's daughter, had flown from California and landed when I was in labor. She is a labor and delivery nurse, arguably one of the best in her area. I wasn't supposed to be in labor for her visit, but I'm glad she and my mother were there for the whole experience. Nearly twenty doctors and nurses were standing outside of the labor room as well, waiting for the worst to happen, but the only unexpected occurrence was David having jaundice, treated only by breast milk and lying under UV lights.

"I have some news," the nurse said as she walked in my room. David was asleep in the little crib by my bed. Swaddled in a white blanket with blue and pink stripes, he looked as peaceful as a three-day old angel. We had nicknamed the room "Club David" due to the shades he had to wear and the blue hue from the UV rays. "The hospital is having to take preventative measures to protect our patients against the coronavirus, so we are no longer allowing visitors. There's even talk of closing down wards because all medical personnel are being redirected to face the incoming emergency of the pandemic. It's about to be an all hands on deck situation."

Oh my goodness . . . this is getting real.

"OK, so what do we do now?" I asked her.

"My advice would be for you and your son to go home and hunker down," she said.

"But he has been diagnosed with jaundice," I said. "Is he OK to leave the hospital or does he need more care?"

"I know, and I have been waiting to speak to the doctors about it," she said, smiling at David as she glanced at him. "We're being pulled all over the place, briefed about what's going on with this disease, ways to protect ourselves from catching it while being surrounded by patients who've been diagnosed with it, and so much more. I will let you know what the doctors say about David as soon as I have some answers. All I know is that it is really bad out there."

"What do you mean?" I asked.

"Everything is shutting down," she said. "Stores, schools, you name it. They're even talking about shutting down borders.

My God, this cannot be happening.

"And who knows for how long," she whispered, shaking her head. "I have family members in other states, and I can't even imagine not being able to see them. My grandmother lives with my aunt in New York and she's very ill and if something were to happen to her and I wasn't there to hold her hand, I just don't know how I'm going to be able to—" she didn't finish. She caught herself before breaking down in tears. "I'm sorry, I shouldn't be saying this to you. You have a beautiful baby boy and it's a happy time for you. I'll go talk to the doctors and will keep you posted on what they say, alright?"

I nodded yes, and she left the room.

I looked at David, who must have been having the most precious dreams because he was smiling in his sleep. Though it warmed my heart, I felt bad for the nurse because she was clearly going through major heartache. *I would be feeling exactly the same way if I were in her shoes.* Fortunately, I had both parents living at home with me, so I wasn't too worried about the borders being closed, but of course I also had friends and other family members sprinkled across the country. And I knew some of them were not in the best health and were considered high risk if, God forbid, they caught this virus.

Wait, did she say that stores were closing down as well?

I sat up as if I had been hit by a lightning bolt. If stores were closing down, who was going to sell Mutt's Sauce? I hadn't checked my emails in days as I had been in full new-mommy mode, pumping milk every two hours, nodding off when David slept, and trying to walk around without overdoing it because I was still quite sore from giving birth. I was about to grab my phone, which had been sitting on the end table by the bed, when—

"Alright, Miss Scales, you and David have been cleared to go home," another nurse said as she walked in with a bunch of paperwork. "David is doing much better with the jaundice, but you still need to keep an eye on him if you see it coming back. We will need to have him come back for a blood test in a couple of days. Here are phone numbers on these papers that you can call and ask for help. Also, don't forget to take care of you and your own recovery. You've just gone through a major change and your body needs time to rest. Keep pumping because it is the best food you can give your son, especially now with this virus going around."

"Yes ma'am," I said, taking the paperwork she had just handed to me.

"Any questions?" she asked with a smile.

A million, but I don't think any of us have the answers just yet.

"No, but thank you for your suggestions," I said.

"Alright, then I'll let you and the baby get ready to leave," she said. "Somebody will come and help you out of the hospital. Do you need a wheelchair, or do you think you're able to walk to the exit?"

"I can walk," I said.

She left the room, and I got out of bed to get to the bag I had brought with me to the hospital. I opened it and looked through its contents to find the outfit I had chosen to put on the baby when it was time to go home. Mom and I packed up the room, anxious to get home and snuggle David 24/7.

Once we made it home, I wanted to take a few days to acclimate before dealing with the tragedy going on in the world and how it affected Mutt's Sauce.

"Since you're pumping milk I can help you with the feedings," my mother suggested.

That's why mothers are irreplaceable. I heard that when a baby is born, people want to go to the hospital to see the baby, but there's one person who goes to the hospital for another reason. It's the mother of the brand-new mother. She goes to the hospital to see her daughter and make sure she's OK, because she's the only one who knows how her daughter feels and what she's going through. That was my mom. I had hit the lottery having Marsha as my mother, and now, as David's grandmother. She had a degree in early childhood education and thirty years of experience in childcare; she was an infant specialist and was also an entrepreneur. Her childcare facility, Masterpiece Learning Center in Cookeville, was so popular, her waitlist was over a year long. Women would literally time their pregnancy with her school openings. Of course, she was over the moon that she had her first grandchild, but she always looked after me too. So, I pumped milk and let her feed David. It was incredible how much that helped me free up time to rest.

But I couldn't rest that much, because notifications on my phone kept reminding me that I had emails to check. Once I finally started going through my emails, I felt as though I was living in a completely different world, one where only action figures like Bruce Willis had lived in. Stores had sent notice of closure, events were being cancelled left and right, food demonstrations were no longer allowed anywhere because it still wasn't clear how the coronavirus traveled and what was contaminated and what was not. I had signed up to attend so many conferences and now not only I couldn't attend, but also suffered from a loss of revenue because they were not issuing any refunds. My entire business model was structured around in-person events, festivals, food demonstrations in store, and conferences.

"What am I going to do to make money?" I asked no one. Well, baby David was by my side, but he was way more interested in chewing on his closed fist than in my serious predicament. "Well, chew all you want, but that house I wanted to buy for us is not going to happen any time soon."

Months prior, soon after discovering that I was expecting a baby, I had decided that I wanted to put down roots and buy a house. The place I currently lived in was a rental and the responsible thing to do was to take the next step and become a homeowner. However, when I went to my banker, she almost laughed in my face.

"Your income is the typical entrepreneurial scenario—a roller coaster," she said, while running the numbers. "Some months are good and some are bad. You're going to have a hard time finding help financing the house."

"So what do I do?" I asked her. "Do I have to look for another job?"

"Yes, but not just any job," she said. "Try to find yourself a good contractor job that will provide you with steady and solid income for the next several months. This is just so we can eventually show banks that you do have a reliable source of revenue that is not dependent upon how well your business does that month."

"But if I take on a full-time job somewhere else, Mutt's Sauce is going to suffer," I said.

She shrugged as if to say, *you can't have your cake and eat it, too.* She was right.

"Listen, once you have a house, you can leave the job if you want and focus back on Mutt's Sauce," she said. "Nobody will care at that point, as long as you keep paying your mortgage, that is."

So, I did as she said and got myself a job as a government contractor. The job came with a great salary, but it was supposed to be temporary. They were gracious enough to give me maternity leave, which I was on in March 2020. However, I was still counting on the money that I made from Mutt's Sauce to allow me to make my dream of home ownership come true. With the pandemic, this was no longer possible, and I found myself not knowing what to do to turn this rock bottom into a trampoline. I mean, how do you tackle the unpredictable?

Since I didn't have the answer to that question, I decided it was time to find it somewhere. I started calling fellow entrepreneurs to see how they were handling the pandemic and what they were doing to ensure their businesses didn't have to shut doors. Then, I told them about my predicament with Mutt's Sauce and the difficulties I was going to have to face when it came to getting through these impossibly hard times.

"You have to shift your business model," one of them said.

"What do you mean?" I asked.

"You're now an in-person type of business, but since we can no longer gather in common spaces, you have to shift it to an online business," he suggested. "Basically, you have to go to e-commerce." I remember the rather hypocritical advice I gave to the young baker. I really didn't think it would ever apply to me.

"But I have no idea how to go about that," I said, my shoulders pushed down by the overwhelming feeling that my business was never going to survive the pandemic.

"Then start looking into it," he said, rather nonchalant, as if he really wanted to say, *You're not going anywhere, what else have you got to do if not to learn about something new?* "You already have a website, right?"

"Yes, but we don't sell sauce from there," I said, desperately wanting him to give me another suggestion that didn't imply I had to completely reinvent how Mutt's Sauce operated.

"Well, then you better start, because it's going to be the only way for you to ride this out," he said.

He's right.

Years before this pandemic, I had a chance to attend an event sponsored by Bunker Labs, a nonprofit organization that provides resources for veteran entrepreneurs and military spouses. They had two titans in business, Gary Vaynerchuk and Matt Higgins, do a Q&A for attendees. I asked them about my business model and scaling in grocery stores. Gary was blunt, pointing out that my business model is backward. "Rather than chasing stores, you need to blow up on e-commerce and have the stores calling you."

Southern parents have a saying, "A hard head makes a soft behind." I am so hardheaded. I gave advice that I didn't even take for myself, and there I was.

As days and weeks went by, I began studying everything I possibly could about e-commerce. For example, I had no idea how to handle packaging and what that process entailed, so I looked up tons of YouTube videos that explained the entire process. Side note: During the pandemic, most people had nothing but time on their hands, so they made countless videos explaining all sorts of stuff. While many Americans were busy learning how to bake bread in a home kitchen, I was busy searching hashtags that dealt with e-commerce (#delivery, #website, #entrepreneurvlog, #foodindustry, #deliveryoptions, #packaging, and so on) and absorbing the information like a sponge, all between diaper changes, feedings, and quick naps.

Four months later, I was making $10,000 a month in online sales. Given that most people were doing their grocery shopping online, the timing of turning my business model into an e-commerce worked very well and I saw an immediate response from the customers.

"Maybe we can buy that house after all," I told my son, who was now more interested in his feet than the prospect of homeownership.

Eventually, I was able to go on QVC and sell Mutt's Sauce. I did the live show of Mutt's Sauce in my own kitchen, on my laptop, which was streamed on QVC. During the demonstration video, I explained the many different ways in which customers could use Mutt's Sauce, not just as a dipping sauce but also as a marinade, perfect for ribs and barbecue seasoning in general. I remember we had about 950 bottles we were hoping to sell, and though I had received positive feedback from the producers of the show, I would have never thought in my wildest dreams that we would *sell out!*

Months prior, I thought the pandemic was going to be the end of my business. Now, I was selling bottles of Mutt's Sauce online like it was going out of style. I couldn't believe it. Not long after our success on QVC, we signed a contract with Lowe's, who agreed to carry our sauce and sell it online as well. Had it not been for the pandemic, I probably would not have thought of turning my business model completely on its head and venture into e-commerce. It's true what they say, necessity is the mother of invention.

A special nod of thanks is owed to my stepfather, Rodney. I like to think of him as the man who stepped up. Mom remarried when I was a pre-teen, and he's always been there for me. He quit his job during the pandemic and learned logistics and packaging to help me turn the business around. We gutted the garage and turned it into an e-commerce fulfillment center. It wouldn't have been possible without him.

SECRET SAUCE: How can entrepreneurs prepare for and handle an unpredictable rock bottom?

Look, I am going to be completely honest with you: There is no way you can prepare for the unpredictable. I mean, how do you go about making a plan to ride out the unforeseeable? But if the pandemic has taught us anything it is that the unpredictable is going to happen—and that most people, specifically Americans, had no idea how to properly wash their hands before COVID hit. The stock market crashing, the terrorist attack at the Twin Towers in 2001, the 2020 coronavirus pandemic. These are all scenarios that shook us at our core. Yet, we survived it. We made do with what we had. We changed the way we handled business. So, how can an entrepreneur turn an unpredictable rock bottom into a trampoline?

Change your business model. You've learned about why and how Mutt's Sauce transitioned from an in-person business model to an e-commerce one. But my business was not the first—nor will it be the last—to shift the business model when necessity came knocking on my door. History is filled with businesses that truly became giants in their field when they decided it was time to make the shift. Netflix went from being a DVD rent-by-mail service, the biggest competitor of Blockbuster, to a streaming service (and most people's best friend during the pandemic). Witnessing the slow, but steady decline of physical media, Netflix made the change in 2007 when it started offering streaming services to the United States. Fast-forward three years and in 2010 Netflix had gone global. Rumor has it that they wanted to begin the streaming service they are so well-known for now much earlier than 2007, but the speed of the internet would not have allowed that model to work just yet.

Another big name that changed the business model is Airbnb. The company went from being a room-rental service to a complete travel experience, which also includes rental properties. Amazon, Uber, Apple, Zoom, Dropbox, and Grubhub are some of the other companies that went through a complete makeover in order to accommodate the new demands and ride out the changing times. If the business model you are currently using no longer fits the way the world is going, don't wait for the world to go back to what it was, because it's never going to happen. I didn't sit around my living room waiting for the pandemic to be over and hope for the best. I had to adjust to the changes—very quick changes, might I add—and so do you. Changing the business model might just be the strategy that prevents your business from becoming a casualty of the next unpredictable rock bottom.

Close your business. Yep, you read that right. It seems as though this one suggestion goes against everything that I have been preaching so far in the book but humor me for a while. I once had a female mentee who unfortunately was dealing with a serious illness—unexpected rock bottom. However, she was so deep into running the business that I noticed she was often going against doctors' orders and not getting the rest she needed to make a speedy and full recovery. So, I decided to confront her about it.

"But I can't quit now because the business needs me," she explained. "If I stop pushing now, then it will send us all the way back to square one and I don't want that to happen."

"I get it," I said, sitting down in front of her. "But you know who else needs you?" I held her hands, looked into her eyes, and said, "your family needs you. They need you more than they need your business. Sure, if you let go of the business now, you'll be starting back from square one and that is so frustrating. A waste of time, money, and energy. I know you don't want that to happen. But what I also know is you don't want to see what happens if you get so sick that you're never going to be able to recover."

She had been looking straight at me, her gaze unwavering, and determination palpable. But when I said that, she lowered her eyes.

"What do I do then?" she said in thin voice.

"Close down the business," I said.

Her eyes looked up again. She was about to say something but decided against it.

"Remember that it's going to be a temporary situation," I said. "Closing down your business does not mean walking away from your business. It means you need to take a break, for whatever reason. When you're ready, you walk back to it and open doors once again."

She nodded.

"Now I need you to leave this conference, go back home, take off your beautiful high heels, and get to bed," I said.

We exchanged a hug, and she followed my suggestion. A year later, she called me up and told me, "I beat it. Let's get back to work!"

And we did.

Like her, so many other entrepreneurs have closed down shops. Some because of personal reasons, others because of financial difficulties, and others of *force majeure*— the unpredictable rock bottom. One of them, Marvel, has been producing some of the biggest blockbuster movies in recent years. But before it became the unstoppable home of larger-than-life American superheroes, Marvel filed for bankruptcy in 1996 after the comic book market and card-trading business were in steady decline. Six Flags, which counts over twenty-five theme parks in their amusement company, also filed for bankruptcy in 2009 because they could not repay their $2.7 billion debt. And of course, as previously mentioned, Daymond John had to shut down his clothing line FUBU four times. Each one of these businesses had to be shut down, but they also reopened bigger and better than before.

So, if an unpredictable rock bottom has you struggling for a solution, perhaps the solution is to walk away from it for a bit to recharge, reorganize, and restructure. Then, come back to it stronger.

Remember your Why. When rock bottom is unpredictable, it can really shake an entrepreneur to their core. When the unthinkable happens, you can find yourself wondering if you'll make it through this rock bottom. Will you have the strength to pivot your business model? Will you have the strength to come back to your business after closing its doors? It is during those truly hard times that the idea of walking away from the entrepreneurial venture once and for all seems to be the best and easiest thing to do. It is when you're at this rock bottom that you have to remember something I addressed at the beginning of the book: your *Why*.

I came close to shutting down Mutt's Sauce more times than I care to admit. Going through a divorce almost pushed me to that point. Drowning in debt almost pushed me to that point. Facing a pandemic almost pushed me to that point. But every single time I faced rock bottom, I closed my eyes and remembered my Why. Charlie "Mutt" Ferrell, Jr., my grandfather. He dedicated his life to three main things: family, service, and bringing people together. The common denominator among these three was the sauce. He used the sauce to bring people together. With his sauce, he broke down racial barriers that still very much existed in the United States Armed Forces when he served. His sauce had witnessed miracles happen: family members who had previously held grudges against one another came together and enjoyed a shared meal made that much more delicious by the sauce; White and Black people sat at the same table as human beings because they shared food they enjoyed, and though they might have had different political and religious views, they surely agreed that sauce was amazing; children finally ate their vegetables without complaining because they could dip carrots and celery sticks in that sauce.

But my grandfather wasn't my only Why. My mother was also my Why. She had raised me all on her own, while living in the projects. I don't know how she did it, but that woman worked multiple jobs and made sure I never missed a Christmas or birthday celebration. She sacrificed her own life just to make sure I could afford an education. It took her eleven—yes, eleven—years to get her bachelor's degree, but she understood the value of leading by example. She is my rock, my strength, my Why.

My grandmother and namesake, Joyce Jean Ferrell, was my Why. I didn't mention her until now because her memory is as raw emotionally as my grandfather's. She was a nurse and military spouse who raised five children while supporting her husband during over twenty years of service. She was the last voice I heard before boarding my first international flight as a new Air Force officer. I called her "Dodie." I must've made it up as a kid because we can't trace the meaning. But she was my heart and my best friend.

Even before David was born, he was my Why. He was the reason why I decided to keep going—I wanted to leave him a legacy he could be proud of. So, to sum it all up, my Why is my family legacy—multiple generations of my family. Every time I came close to shutting down Mutt's Sauce once and for all, I remembered my grandfather, grandmother, my mother, and also my son. They're my Why. As long as I have my family, I will always have a reason not to give up. Find your Why. Sometimes, your Why is all you have to hold on to. But that Why will be strong enough to carry you through the most unpredictable of rock bottoms and turn it into the most incredible trampoline.

ROCK BOTTOM HAS A TRAMPOLINE

"**M**om, you're never going to believe what just happened," I told my mother as I walked from my office to the kitchen where she had been cooking dinner. "I got the email of a lifetime!"

"What email?" my mom asked, mixing a fresh salad.

"Well, Daymond John's team reached out to me saying that he's writing a new book that will talk about how to take charge of your life and create the future of your dreams. He'll be featuring stories from entrepreneurs who've done just that and they're currently gathering stories that have the potential of making it into the book." I took a deep breath to make the big reveal. "They want to interview me."

"Oh my! That's amazing!" she said, giving me a hug.

"I can't believe it," I said with the biggest smile on my face. "I mean, I know that my story might not make it into the final book, but just to be asked means everything to me."

"Yes, you should be very proud of that," my mom said as she sprinkled a bit more salt and mixed some more. "So, what are the next steps?"

"They'll schedule a call with his team, and we'll go from there. I can't believe this is all happening at once," I said, placing both hands on my stomach. I had only recently found out that I was going to be a mother. "From what I understand my due date is a day before the projected release date for the book!"

"Look at God," my mom said, placing the salad bowl on the table along with a bottle of Mutt's Sauce.

A few weeks later, I was at a conference in Ohio that Daymond John was also attending. There, I took the opportunity to share some very personal and important news with him. I told him I was pregnant.

"Congratulations!" he said.

I didn't tell him that he was the third person to whom I had revealed the pregnancy news—aside from my parents, nobody else knew. You couldn't really see my belly just yet, so had I not said anything he would not have been able to tell. But he had been such a positive presence in my life lately that I felt like I wanted and needed to share that with him. What also inspired me to share the news with him was the way he ended the speech he gave at the conference. He talked about legacy and how important that is. For the first time in my life, the word *legacy* had taken on a whole new meaning. That was the moment when it clicked for me that I was no longer running Mutt's Sauce just to do right by grandfather and keep his legacy alive. Now I was an entrepreneur because I wanted to leave a legacy to my child, to the future of Mutt's Sauce.

Soon after our meeting, I spoke to his team, shared my story, told them I had seen Daymond John at the conference, and that I had given him the scoop of my pregnancy—which I planned on announcing to my community at the Military Influencer Conference in Washington, D.C., that September, where I was scheduled to deliver a keynote speech. After our chat, weeks went by, and I didn't hear anything else from them. Well, you could have knocked me over with a feather when I found out that they had not only chosen my story to be in *Powershift*, but they had dedicated a whole chapter to me![8] As I began reading the book, I was truly humbled by the way Daymond John had described me and my journey. To see myself through somebody else's lens—somebody I deeply admire—was like I was learning something new about myself.

As I sat there, with his book open on my desk—my name written among others that I consider to be giants in the world of entrepreneurship, such as Mark Cuban, Kris Jenner, and tennis legend Billy Jean King—I couldn't help but think of all the years I spent with my head down working hard to accomplish my dream of entrepreneurship, and the many obstacles I had to overcome in both my personal and professional life. *Rock bottom does indeed have a trampoline.*

Each rock bottom almost broke me.

The divorce almost broke me as a woman, but I turned it into a trampoline when I decided to use the lessons learned to re-evaluate my life, reorder my priorities, and become the woman I was always meant to be. Being surrounded by like-minded people almost broke me both as a woman and as an entrepreneur, but the trampoline moment happened when I understood the importance of surrounding myself with like-hearted people. The debt almost broke me, once again both personally and professionally, but I learned so much from my mistakes and I don't believe I would be financially literate today had it not been for that rock bottom. The pandemic had the potential to break me, on multiple levels. Instead, I turned that rock bottom into a trampoline when I used the forced time off to enjoy motherhood. Who knows how much time I could have spent with my baby had I been traveling around the country to promote Mutt's Sauce. But when the

---

8. Daymond John with Daniel Paisner, *Powershift: Transform Any Situation, Close Any Deal, and Achieve Any Outcome* (New York: Currently, 2021).

pandemic closed the world for months, I was given the most wonderful and precious gift of all: time with my son.

I had to lose nearly everything to finally get everything.

You might be going through one of the hardest things you have ever faced, either as an individual or a professional, or perhaps both. But don't give up. Remember that diamonds are born from pressure. There is always the opportunity to grow, no matter how hard the lesson is. All you need to do is to be willing to learn that lesson. Once you do, you will know how to turn the rock bottom you're facing into the trampoline that is going to help you grow as a person and as an entrepreneur. And when it all gets to be too much, look for your *Why* and grab ahold of it. Don't ever let go of it.

My Why is now multifaceted, but I will always remember that it started with my mother and grandfather. And to them, I say *thank you*. Thank you for raising me and for teaching me the values I grew up with and that I now pass on to my son. To my grandfather: Thank you for showing me the importance of serving our country. Thank you for trusting me with your recipe. All these years later, you're still breaking barriers, reuniting family members, and bringing people together with your sauce. To my mother: God outdid Himself by putting me in your care. Thank you for your unconditional support and always being my number one fan. You believed in me when I didn't even believe in myself. And to you, reader, I hope this testimony was everything you hoped, and I implore you to share your story when the time comes. Just reach out. And keep going. I believe in you.

ACKNOWLEDGEMENTS

David Dewayne: You are lying next to me sleeping peacefully as I write this and let the tears fall. Dreams of you kept me here. It's been like an invisible thread, pulling me forward year after year. My whole adult life, visions of you danced in my head. At times, I didn't want to wake up and face a reality that didn't have you in it. Life before you felt like a question mark, and now it's an exclamation. Your eyes remind me of your great-grandmother, almost like she personally picked your soul for me. Your rowdy and protective spirit is a reminder of the headstrong men who came before you. Your sweet, dimpled smile, I'm reminded, is a replica of your grandmother's. You're not just my legacy. Sharing you with the world was the proudest and most terrifying moment of my life. I pray this world is kind to you. The prayers of your ancestors will cover you. And finally, I ask God to be gracious enough to let me stay for as long as possible so I can witness your journey. My beautiful baby boy. You're my greatest accomplishment. Mama loves you.

Joyce Jean Ferrell, aka Dodie: I learned somewhere that if a woman gives birth to a girl, she not only gave birth to her, but also her grandchildren. I've always felt a closeness to you I couldn't describe as a child. I learned later in life that you loved to write. I've carried you with me always. This is your book, too. Hug Uncle Frankie, Uncle Chuck, and Aunt Glenda for me. Charlynda Jean.

Mom: My undisputed biggest fan. Thank you for saving every drawing, photo, or scribble I made. Thank you for sending me to all the programs. Thank you for listening to my tall tales from school. Thank you for driving five hours in the middle of the night and randomly showing up to my dorm because you "just knew I missed you." Thank you for loving me through my mistakes. Thank you for telling me you loved and believed in me during times when, unbeknownst to you, I was struggling to stay. Thank you for leading by example, not only in life, but in your unwavering faith in God. You'll always smell like butterflies. I love you, Mama.

Papa: My only regret is giving you a hard time when you first stepped up to take care of my mother and I. You were the answer to many prayers. When I look at the hardest times in my life, you were always a steady source of calm. I never worried if Mom would be OK, because she had you. The older I get, the deeper my gratitude is for you and your love. Thank you for the limo rides and ice cream. Love you, Papa.

The Ferrell-Apple-Burnley-Allen family and all our descendants: Growing up, I may have had a different last name, but I knew what family I belonged to. May you all be blessed eternally.

My brothers, Carlos and Dewon: I never felt like the two of you were cousins. Thank you for looking out for me, from protecting me from kindergarten bullies, to entertaining my letters from science camp (sorry Dewon!), to catching cotton mouth snakes, to pulling me off the dance floor at my first outing to a nightclub because, "I don't belong there"— you two were the siblings I needed. I love you.

Mi prima, **Tasha:** The timing of your arrival for the birth of David was no coincidence. When I was in my most vulnerable state, you were right by my side. Motherhood has always been your calling. *Los amo Tia Carmen, Abuela, Max y la familia California!*

Uncle Dewayne: Your legacy had to live on. What can I say to the man who was my first male superhero? Thank you for being so fun, and for showing me life outside of my little town. Thank you for not throwing in the towel after my first trip to Charleston (ha!). Thank you for entertaining my big ideas, and for following your dreams so I could see what was possible. Thank you for your service and for joining the Navy. Lord knows I couldn't swim. Thank you for living your life unapologetically. Thank you for calling and talking to David Dewayne every day. Love you more than turnip greens and hot water cornbread.

Uncle Jamie: I see you. I acknowledge you. I love you.

Shout out to Ricco, too: I see you cuz!

Brenda and C4: Although bittersweet, one of the greatest blessings of my adult life is the ability to say I've even met you. I love you, my sweet cousins.

Nneda: A special shoutout to the only human I've ever seen that felt like looking into a mirror other than my own child. May God protect and watch over you always.

All my many Aunties, like Aunt Missy, Aunt Karen, Aunt Vickeyyyyyy, and Aunt Carolyn: Thank you for letting me adopt you. Your support has been immeasurable and invaluable.

My childhood Cookeville friends, especially: Jessica, Seth, Melissa, Brittany, Nick, Lacey, Tonya, Amber, Rose, Katie, and Carlos L. Thank you for giving me memories I can look back on fondly. I'm glad many of us are still in touch. Your love and support keep me grounded.

To the Copelands: Dr. Scott, Mona, Hayden, Blair, Morgan, Tate and Papa Steve. Thank you for your trust above all else. Your family taught me invaluable lessons over the years. Mainly, family doesn't have to be blood related. I love y'all.

My KTP sisters: Viola, Aubrey, Erin, Heidi, and Nicole. We've officially been friends for more years than we haven't. Thank you for being one of my only true safe spaces. If anything happens, please delete everything. Sparkles!! Chuck.

To all the parents and children who supported or attended Masterpiece Learning Center: your trust in my mother and the smiles on their faces impacted me more than you know. Thank you.

My military tribe, especially the WarTown crew, Wright Patt crew, Phil Fantastic, David De La Rue and the SF crew in Texas, General CD Moore, Bunker Labs, Military Influencer Conference, military spouses and veteran entrepreneur crew, MAFO, MVA, MPU, VPI, and other brothers and sisters in arms I've bonded with on this entrepreneurial journey . . . one team, one fight. I'm here for you, always. Thank you for your service and thank you for the bonds that built me.

To all my mentees that took my (sometimes hypocritical) advice: You're gonna make it. Thank you for trusting me. The honor was mine and little did you know, I was also taking notes from you.

To my Clemson University and Clemson athletics friends: C-U-U-KNOW!!

To Janine: I had no idea your phone call would be the wake-up call that led to this book. Thank you for being a glass ceiling shatterer, an unpaid therapist, and the host of life changing things you did in the span of twenty minutes. You're amazing beyond words.

To MollyJean: I'm thoroughly convinced we were twins separated at birth. It's all a conspiracy. Seriously, you're my heart. In the end, my prayer is that we will meet in some remote part of the country as old ladies and chuckle as we rock on a porch and recount the memories of how we survived all the things we know have happened. Tag—your turn to tell your story. Love you to the moon and back. CharlyndaMae

The Sedlocks: Just like the Copelands, family can be whoever your heart deems is that close. That's you. You're my family. Thank you for your unconditional love and support. Thank you for increasing my credit score. And Mom says thanks for the delicious recipes. Love you.

To Tiye: If anyone understands the art of the bounce back, it's you, Sis. Your testimony is as powerful as your megawatt smile. Thank you for your service. Keep going.

To my sister Maria: You're my happy thought through it all. You are enough. You deserve all the good things. Thank you for staying in a time when I felt I lost a whole family. I love you forever.

To Bhakti: Our sisterhood was unexpected and the greatest blessing. You're the only mom friend I really had during a time when I didn't even know how to be a mom. Thank you for writing your story, which truly inspired me. Thank you for loving and leaping, which also inspires me. Thank you for sharing your children so David could have friends. The sky's the limit, Colonel. I'm just glad to have a front row seat.

To Tchoia: Whatever part of the world you're in, please believe my heart is there with you. Thank you for being the sister I never knew I needed. Thank you for letting me be an aunt to the most beautiful angels. Ain't no ocean, ain't no sea . . .

To Holly and my Beavercreek sisters: I dare say I wouldn't be here if it weren't for the likes of you ladies. I had no clue what I was doing as an entrepreneur. Thank you for understanding the spirit of collaboration, referrals, mentorship, and friendship. Thank you for including me, even when you knew I was stretched so thin my answer may be 'no' more than a few times. Thank you for not gatekeeping. Thank you for keeping it real.

Fawn Freeman: I've never been so grateful for a supervisor. I've never cried at work. I've never hugged a supervisor or been hugged with such genuine concern like that day in your office. Thank you for never settling for a lesser version of me. Thank you for taking a chance on me. Thank you for showing me what top-notch performance looked like. Thank you for your honesty—about life. It's the only job I ever worked where I truly didn't want to leave. I'm so glad we're still friends. You deserve every bit of your retirement and decades more of rest and family time.

RoShawn Saunders: The man with the divine vision. I am still baffled at how, in one try, you executed the logo for Mutt's Sauce and captured my grandfather's spirit so perfectly. I no longer question why some people came into my life. It is crystal clear why you were there.

Jacqueline Neal for coaching me through *Shark Tank* and the years of support following that. If you tell me to jump, I'm there. I'm glad I ran to that stage. You're a blessing.

John Soutar, Peggy Hein Bellamy, SCORE mentors, the Beavercreek and Dayton Chambers of Commerce, and the first Mutt's Sauce board of advisors: Your guidance and resources are a masterclass on mentorship. Thank you for helping me move at the speed of determination. I've dedicated my life to paying it forward. My prayer is that it's even half as valuable as the help you gave me. God bless you.

Girl Scouts of the USA: My journey to serving others was honed by your values. Thank you for the sisterhood, for not kicking me out when I nearly burned down a lodge getting my cooking badge, and for providing me with lifelong bonds I am proud to talk about decades later.

My favorite teacher, Mrs. Sue Pecora: As a country girl who lived in the projects, I didn't know my fourth grade teacher was going to impact me as greatly as you did. The day you showed us "expensive food" like caviar and escargot opened the world. It wasn't just snails and fish eggs. It was, "There's so much more outside of Cookeville." Thank you for daring me to dream big.

Authors who have shared my story in their own books, like Daymond John and The Shark Group, Nicholas Battle,

Todd Connor, Lisa Kipps-Brown, and "Iron" Mike Steadman. Additionally, anyone who's ever shared my story and that of Mutt's Sauce—you didn't have to do it, and for that, I'm grateful. It gave me the bravery to share this story.

Jamaica, Dabriah, and team of OH Taste Foundation: In the midst of chaos was clarity. Our mission is also bigger than us. You're the like-hearted people I'd prayed for in this phase of life. With you, we can achieve anything. Thank you for your hard work and most importantly, your friendship.

To the Mutt's Sauce family, specifically the Kroger crew: Your friendship is so great it almost seems mythical. None of this book would exist without the part you played in getting Mutt's Sauce on the shelf. More than that, you opened my eyes to facets of friendship that my grandfather spoke about: bonds that don't require you to have the same age or background. I can't even begin to recall a favorite memory; they were all that great. I pray time is kind so we can make even more. My humblest thanks.

I talked a lot about my divorce and my relationship with a former assistant. I want to publicly acknowledge that not all the memories were bad.

Gratitude flows from the deepest recesses of my heart to those who have brought this book to life. Behind these pages is a tapestry of dedication, collaboration, and unwavering support that has shaped my journey as an author.

To Brunella, my extraordinary ghostwriter and owner of The Military Editor® Agency, your ability to capture my voice and breathe life into my thoughts is a gift beyond measure. You have translated my ideas into a symphony of words that resonate with authenticity, and for that, I am profoundly grateful.

To JuLee Brand and W. Brand Publishing, your belief in the power of this narrative has paved the way for its realization. Your willingness to take a chance on this project is a testament to your dedication to meaningful storytelling. Your guidance, expertise, and unwavering enthusiasm have infused this endeavor with purpose and promise.

This book is not merely a collection of words on paper; it's a manifestation of the countless hours, sleepless nights, and shared dreams that have culminated in its existence. Your impact is immeasurable to all those who provided encouragement, insights, and valuable contributions along the way.

As I reflect on the culmination of this endeavor, I am reminded that the power of collaboration and unity can transcend the pages of a book. Together, we have birthed an idea into reality, and prayerfully, a movement of authenticity and deeper connections.

Finally, I extend my deepest thanks to the Divine, who has been my steadfast companion throughout the trials of hitting rock bottom. Just as the first verse in the book of James reminds us that trials can lead to perseverance, I have witnessed how challenges have shaped my journey and strengthened my spirit. Your presence has been my refuge, providing solace when hope seemed distant and fortitude when I faced adversity. My heartfelt appreciation goes to the guiding force that has helped me navigate the depths and rise from rock bottom.

In unwavering faith,
Charlynda Nyenke Scales

CHARLYNDA SCALES is a serial entrepreneur: She serves as founder and CEO of Mutt's Sauce LLC and OH Taste LLC; Executive Director of the OH Taste Foundation (501c3).

A sought-after speaker and coach for women's empowerment and small businesses, she is a TEDx speaker. Her talent is cultivating influential people by meeting them where they are in life and business. Her military career spans over fifteen years; she's currently an Air Force Reservist stationed at Wright Patterson Air Force Base in Ohio.

Mutt's Sauce and Charlynda have been featured in *Yahoo! Finance, NPR, Forbes.com, QVC, Men's Journal, CBS News, NBCUniversal, Black Enterprise Magazine,* and *Military.com,* among others.

Charlynda was also featured in FUBU Founder and *Shark Tank* investor Daymond John's bestselling book, *Powershift*.

She is a Clemson University graduate with a degree in Aerospace Science and Business Management. She also holds an MBA in Strategic Leadership. She started the company Mutt's Sauce, LLC while still serving on active duty in the military. She is a graduate of the following distinguished courses: Tuck School of Executive Leadership at Dartmouth, The Empower Program, by Dayton Chamber of Commerce, The Course for Presidents, by Aileron, Executive Education, Harvard Kennedy School.

Charlynda currently sits on the board of Bunker Labs, Veterans for Political Innovation, and Dayton Convention and Visitors Bureau. She is a Gold Award Winner and has a Lifetime Membership to Girl Scouts of the USA. She is one of 25 Americans highlighted as We are the Mighty's Class of 2022.

Her son, David, is, in her opinion, her finest achievement.

Printed in the USA
CPSIA information can be obtained
at www.ICGtesting.com
LVHW071500031123
762897LV00021B/1341